What people are

MW01248956

"Teamability: Role-fit + Team-fit + coherent teaming = Focused and happy employees + profits and success."

Roy Brittany Blacklidge ~ President & CEO, Blacklidge Emulsions

"Whether you have hiring quality problems, or team performance problems, or any other people-related issues or challenges, stop paying so much attention to 'talent,' and focus on finding the right team players."

Mike O'Neill ~ Founder & CEO, Preferred Sands

"Janice, you didn't just create a new technology. You created a whole new field of management science."

Stephen M. Goodman ~ Senior Partner and founder of the emerging business and technology law practice, Morgan Lewis

"Every human being should have the gift of knowing how they team and what their innate approaches to work are. Teamability has the ability to save them a lot of unnecessary toil and disappointment; all while bringing clarity and focus to their life's work."

Janine N. Truitt ~ Chief Innovations Officer, Talent Think Innovations, LLC

"Teamability is an invaluable resource. The reports are especially helpful as we work to understand individual team members and the team as a whole. We use Teamability to focus natural talents and Roles to achieve operational goals. Thank you, DrJanice!"

Jonathan Barnes ~ CEO, Staffing As A Mission

"Dr. Janice Presser provides refreshing, direct and powerful insight into the challenges that leaders and teams face in today's world. Her background of theoretical and real life experience applies an essential cranial defibrillator to anyone serious about creating and leading enabled teams."

Harry Tucker ~ Fortune 25 Strategy Advisor / Global Technology Architect

"Teamability is like having the answer key to a million-piece organizational puzzle."

R 'Ray' Wang ~ Principal Analyst & Founder, Constellation Research

"Rarely is an individual's vision so closely matched with what they ultimately deliver. Dr. Presser has consistently surpassed the mark. Her discoveries around teams and workforce dynamics are truly game-changing."

Darryl King ~ Discipleship Pastor, Lake Norman Baptist Church; Board of Directors, Christianity Today

"I read my Teamability Leader's Playbook yesterday and could not be more thrilled. It is the ultimate reference guide. This will literally save years of trial and error, learning what makes people tick and how to get the most out of them. Now I can skip the chase and get on with the business of being in business. Thank you, a million times over!"

Paul Johnson ~ Director of Logistics, Blacklidge Emulsions, Inc.

"The notion of people having strategic value is broadly categorized as an art more than a science. But now, through Teamability, DrJanice helps us all understand human strategic value scientifically."

Richie Etwaru ~ Chief Digital Officer, QuintilesIMS

"Dr. J's approach to employee selection, placement and team development is a valuable asset to our company as we focus on culture change to facilitate our growth and sustainability in the future. The easily understood, easily translatable, and easily applied 'where the rubber meets the road' tools, insight and support are valuable components of our quest."

Ernie Inmon ~ Chairman and CEO, U.S. Axle, Inc.

"Teamability has the potential to minimize friction within a company, enabling teams to solve problems and build internal resilience. If you are a leader, you simply must see what this technology can do to propel you forward, faster."

Natalie Neelan ~ Business Innovation Strategy Consultant, Highmark

@DrJanice

Timing Isn't Everything.
Teaming Is.

More on Leadership and Teamwork
from the Creator of Teamability®

Dr. Janice Presser
Foreword by R 'Ray' Wang

Team well and Prosper!
Best,
Dr. J

TEN TREES PRESS
Philadelphia

Copyright © 2017 by Dr. Janice Presser.
All rights reserved.

ISBN: 978-0-9898012-2-5

No part of this book may be reproduced in any form or by any
electronic or mechanical means, including information storage and retrieval
systems, without permission in writing from the publisher, except by
a reviewer who may quote brief passages in a review.

Originally published in paperback — May, 2017 — by Ten Trees Press
P. O. Box 1396, Doylestown, PA 18901

Editing: Mark Talaba
Graphic Design & Production: Jerad MacLean (CanyonGraphicArts.com)
Photography: Tom Thomson
Illustrations: © The Gabriel Institute

Printed in the United States of America

For the team.

Always in my heart.

@DrJanice

Contents

Foreword

Organizations embarking on the journey of digital transformation face challenges not only in creating disruptive business models, but also in constantly pursuing the art of the possible. The intensity of transformational innovation demands teams of digital artisans who can balance each other out, and from more than just a left-brain/right-brain perspective.

Why? Because the art of the possible calls for a design thinking approach. Design thinking is complex: simultaneously systemic and intuitive; logical and non-linear. It seeks questions that have never been asked, and solutions that have never existed. Success requires team diversity, but not as defined by traditional markers of age, gender, race, religion, or sexual orientation. Rather, the digital DNA required to thrive in an ongoing state of ambiguity and discovery can only be found through diversity of teaming qualities amongst team members.

Technology that identifies and organizes the elements of teaming now exists. It was created by Dr. Janice Presser and The Gabriel Institute. Moreover, organizations can apply this technology to attract, develop, and sustain high performing teams.

Visionary leaders know that in order to achieve lasting competitive advantage, they need to build sustainable cultures of innovation. Unfortunately, the desired results don't necessarily arise from a gathering of skills, education, prior experience, intelligence, drive, or other familiar human abilities and attributes. But they can, and do, arise wherever high-quality, high-clarity teaming ability reaches critical mass.

To prepare for a new team-centric future, leaders must master the ground rules of teaming, which are identified in this, Dr. Janice's latest book, 'Timing Isn't Everything. Teaming Is.' Through anecdotes, examples, lessons, and personal musings, she cultivates awareness of sound, science-based teaming concepts and practices that can ensure short term and long term team success. Applying these methods will dramatically improve the odds for survival in a world where organizations must disrupt… or be disrupted.

Here's to a successful teaming journey ahead!

R 'Ray' Wang

Principal Analyst & Founder, Constellation Research
Author of *Disrupting Digital Business: Create an Authentic Experience in the Peer-to-Peer Economy*, HBR Press 2015

Introduction

I never envisioned a sequel to *@DrJanice: Thoughts & Tweets on Leadership, Teamwork & Teamability*®. Like many things in life that you don't know are important – till you see them in the rearview mirror…while trying not to run them over – it just happened.

And that's all related to the 'why' of this book. It happened because the TGI Team needed it to happen. But when I say 'Team,' I don't mean just a group of people who share their work and collaborate and thus are expected to be engaged and productive and all that.

When I say Team, I mean the living, breathing entity that comes into being when people join together to achieve a common purpose. This kind of Team has a life of its own, animated by the people who are moved to serve its needs, even as we go about fulfilling our various personal missions every day.

The TGI Team needed for its Founder – that's the person who feeds everyone with the inspiration to keep plugging away, believing that future will be better and brighter for everyone – to do a refresh on the ideas that brought this Team into being; ideas that can change the world.

So, like a good laborer, I did what management – the Team – asked of me.

I hope you find it enlightening, useful, inspiring, or whatever else will help you fulfill your mission in life.

Team Well and Prosper!

DrJ

March 30, 2017

@DrJanice: To understand passion, look at extreme sports – like skydiving, or leading an entrepreneurial team.

Part 1: Timing

This is a small book, and I do a lot of talking in it, so just to balance that out, here are some thoughts about time and timing from other people, all of diverse backgrounds and great achievements.

"No matter how busy you are, you must take time to make the other person feel important."

— *Mary Kay Ash*

"Yesterday, today was tomorrow."

— *James McPhillips, and others*

"Better three hours too soon than a minute too late."

— *William Shakespeare*

"Yesterday's the past, tomorrow is a mystery, and today is a gift. That's why they call it the present."

— *Eleanor Roosevelt*

"We must use time as a tool, not as a crutch."

— *John F. Kennedy*

"There comes a time when the world gets quiet and the only thing left is your own heart. So you'd better learn the sound of it. Otherwise you'll never understand what it's saying."

— *Sarah Dessen*

"Time flies like an arrow; fruit flies like a banana."

— *Groucho Marx*

"Time is a great teacher. But unfortunately, it kills all of its students."

— *Hector Berlioz*

@DrJanice: You can't help everyone. But you can buy them a cup of coffee. And serve it up with grace, because that's even more important than the caffeine.

I love Harry Potter and his friends. And I love the teachers at Hogwarts, even the ones who are a little scary. Because secretly, I wish my school had taught me the basics: how to talk to owls (and other wildlife, including many humans); how to do battle with the forces that other people (besides you) don't always see; and how to be a great team player (and not just for Quidditch, either) even when the other side has bigger kids on it. Because that, in essence, is what adulthood has required of me.

"If I only had the Sorting Hat..."

Excitement is swirling about the new Harry Potter film being released this November. More properly, it's a prequel, since it takes place long before Harry's parents were born, but a lot of us Potter fans are getting our Hogwarts on, anyway. (I'm summoning my inner Hermione and yes, thank you, I was very much like her as a child – minus the wand and the incantations.)

So a few weeks ago, that was my state of mind while I was having a therapeutic cup of coffee with the head of Talent Acquisition at a very large company, whom I'll call 'Tracy.' At least the headache-du-jour was not the common problem of attracting applicants. Tracy had nailed that one, years ago. Admittedly, it's less of a challenge when your company is pretty much a household name. And branding as a preferred employer hadn't been much of a concern either, for the same reason.

"It's a little like Hogwarts," Tracy said, referencing the School of Witchcraft and Wizardry where Harry and his friends began their adventures. "You get these amazing people who come in the door with the natural ability and all the right qualifications, and I expect that they'll fit right in, become full-fledged business wizards, and work some magic on behalf of the team. Their managers proceed with the same hopes and expectations, but the crazy stuff that sometimes happens next is totally beyond me."

It's a natural assumption that gaining entry to a world of money and prestige and opportunities and perks is a sure-fire path to employee happiness, engagement, and retention. But Tracy was clearly worried that lasting success in these matters might just be an illusion, like the ones that so often complicated Harry Potter's world.

So, summoning up my past life as a therapist, I asked, 'What do you think would change all that?' (You can lead a shrink to 'retirement' but you can't make her stop wanting to help people.)

Said Tracy, "If I only had the Sorting Hat…"

Perhaps you don't have more than a passing recollection of Harry Potter and the whole Hogwarts experience, so I'll spell this part out for you. ("Spell." Get it? Ok, if you don't, Google 'JK Rowling.')

The Sorting Hat, over a thousand years ago, belonged to one of the founders of Hogwarts. In the beginning, it was just a hat. But over the centuries, it took on a life of its own (as things in magical places sometimes do) and became the resident expert in assigning new students to one of the four 'Houses' of Hogwarts – the one with characteristics and culture that would be best suited for a particular wizard-to-be.

Sounds a bit like what Talent Acquisition seeks to accomplish, doesn't it? No doubt that's what Tracy was thinking.

So how did the Sorting Hat work?

Well, it didn't test for a range of skills, or knowledge, or cleverness, or any single attribute in particular.

The Sorting Hat actually interacted with the person upon whose head it was placed. Some clearly sensed this, and even tried to converse with it. Others were less aware – perhaps a predictor of the way in which they would approach, and (dare I say?) team with their colleagues.

The Sorting Hat never rejected anyone. It merely sorted them into the environment within which they would be most likely to succeed. That's because the Hat was beholden to the vision of Hogwarts. And for a vision to be sustained, it needs to be served well.

The result, at Hogwarts, was pretty remarkable, when you consider how quickly and easily readers (and, later, viewers) learned to identify who belonged to which House.

I couldn't help but explain to Tracy that there really is a Sorting Hat, of a sort. It's not like the one that sent Harry and Hermione and Ron to the House of Gryffindor. It can't speak out loud, but it can write. And it really does identify the way a person seeks to serve team needs, what kind of job responsibilities they are most likely to enjoy, and also the kinds of teaming and business contexts that will bring out the best in them.

And as you've probably guessed, it lives at our house.

p.s. You can access and apply this modern Sorting Hat – Teamability® – and you won't need a wand, or an owl, or a potion. Your phone or email will do nicely. Call us at +1.215.825.2500 or send email to clients@thegabrielinstitute. com.

@DrJanice: Meaningful work isn't a Constitutionally guaranteed right. Maybe it should be. #peace #harmony #teaming

Maybe it's just an artifact of being a Baby Boomer, but I have many young friends who feel as I do, that work is central to the well-lived life. For us, it's the source of meaningful, productive relationships that let us do more than we could ever do alone. That said, it wasn't always that way, and maybe it never will be for many people. I wish, sometimes, that I could legislate job satisfaction. When people enjoy their work, they are better with their families, friends, neighbors – and I think that extends to the world. (Yes, I marched for peace in the sixties. Haven't given up on it yet.)

What I Learned From My First Seven Jobs

There's a meme making its way around the web in which people name their first seven jobs. Such recollections often involve typical teenage ventures like mowing lawns and selling lemonade. Sometimes people even brand them as 'my first entrepreneurial journey,' or claim to have gained great insight from the experience. I won't. Because the fact is, I really did not want to do any of my first seven. I didn't do them for love. At the time, I was strictly in it for the money.

That doesn't mean I can't recast them now, in the light of how I might have (with stress on 'might') learned something that's now indispensable to my business self. Can't say with any honesty that any of these jobs were truly meaningful, to me, or the world, in any way. Certainly none of them were even remotely as soul-fulfilling as what I'm doing now.

First job: Babysitter. I was thirteen, and 'teen' was my primary qualification. Well, that, plus my ability to play the gender card. Babysitting, perhaps the only job in which girls were the preferred candidates over boys, was easy to get...especially in the summer. It consisted mainly of sitting on the porch, swatting mosquitos, reading trashy novels, and hoping that all the kids stayed asleep – and I stayed awake – until the parents came home.

Lesson learned: Taking care of other people's kids is boring. (Note to self: do not try to manage interns when you can get someone else to do it.)

Second, I was an office girl. That is not a misprint. It was an actual job title. The office girl was the one who was expected to answer the phone and smile. She was not expected to lift packages or get within a mile of any heavy machinery. Ok, so there are tradeoffs in everything. I did learn the fundamentals of bookkeeping, pre-QuickBooks.

Lesson learned: It is important to know who the real boss is. In family companies, it's the guy whose name is on the papers in the locked file, not the one you report to who you call 'Mister' and everyone else calls 'Sonny.' Unless, that is, his name really is Sonny.

Third, I was a bookkeeping assistant. Now, to dissuade anyone who's thinking, "Aha, she really knows how to build a resume," I want you to know I got this job because the overworked bookkeeper was my aunt. (Side note: the previous job was gotten because a friend of mother's wanted to take the whole summer off. They really wanted her to come back, so they agreed. I don't know what she told them about me, but I suspect she added a few years to my real age – fifteen at the time.)

Lesson learned: If you make a bookkeeping mistake, you absolutely, positively, have to correct it. Because in some areas of business, there are no secrets. (I learned some other stuff in that job too, about boys who were planning to be the Sonny in their dad's business, but that stuff is not for this publication at this time.)

So I had gained real experience in the world of business. I knew how to calculate taxes and manage a payroll, where the most important thing was getting the right amount in each pay envelope. I knew how to write a deposit slip for my bank account, which paid interest. And I knew that I needed to graduate college because no way was I ever going to learn to type.

My fourth job really wasn't much of a job, in that it had no other requirement than being a college freshman. But it brought in more money than babysitting, so it counts. The job consisted of being an experimental psychology subject. And here I came away with more than just cash. I figured out their trade secret!

Lesson learned: No matter how authoritative someone looks, do not believe them until they have proved themselves to be unassailably trustworthy. (This was quite useful in a time when 'question authority' and 'don't trust anyone over 30' were wildly popular slogans of youth culture.)

Fifth job (so soon?): A couple of college instructors had a side gig finding smart young people to do intensely boring work that required high-level reading ability. The job was called 'Survey Answer Coder' and yes, I qualified. In fact, I was probably close to the edge of being overqualified, at least in the reading dimension.

Lesson learned: Just because you can do something doesn't mean that you should. Because life is short, and bored is a terrible way to live. Even for a four-hour shift.

Next in line – I took on the job of a nanny, making my sixth job the first one I ever accepted, even though I knew I would hate it. Now if you have been reading attentively, you know that I was not a great match for babysitting. But I was in college, I needed money, and I was still a girl. Who couldn't type.

Lesson learned: Job title does not matter. How you are expected to interact with other people, including children, matters. A lot.

Mercifully, I finally graduated. My major in psychology qualified me for two jobs. One was 'research assistant,' which meant I would have to type at least 35 words a minute. (Apparently most non-typists could do this, as long as they knew the alphabet.) I ended up doing the other one because it paid more and typing was optional.

And so my seventh job was as a social worker in a major city with more than its share of social problems. I don't think I solved any, although I know that in some people's minds, I probably added to them. Turned out that social change or benefit wasn't even on my employer's agenda, so I joined the union and helped organize.

Lesson learned: The lesser of two evils is still evil. And evil includes not being able to make meaningful contributions to something bigger than yourself.

I am, of course, a lot older now. And maybe even a tad wiser. There have been a lot of jobs between number 7 and the one I have now. While those lessons learned in my youth are still valid, I now have a much bigger context in which to put them. That context is teaming: understanding it, doing it, and sharing it.

The lessons are simple. And like many good things, they come in three.

1. People do best what they like best and they like best what they do best. No matter how smart and talented you are, you are still not an exception.

2. If there is not enough excitement in what you do – or if there is too much, in which case you will feel it as stress – you will neither enjoy it nor be able to give it your best.

3. The more your job requires you to interact with others – whether they be managers, fellow employees, customers, or other stakeholders – in ways that don't feel right, or that you do not value, the less you will feel good about yourself.

Keep these three lessons front and center, and you'll likely discover the secret of happiness. Because if you've never had them all going for you, maybe your real job is being an entrepreneur.

@DrJanice: As soon as you start calling yourself a #leader, you're probably failing at it.

If you want to expand your spheres of knowledge, hang out with people who are not like you. (Consider not only what they look like, but how they think and what they know about.) And, most important, listen to them! That's how I put two and two together and figured out that one of my most important skills was knowing how to fail.

Make Failing a Daily Habit

You didn't read that wrong. And if you're looking for a rah-rah success read, you're on the wrong page.

I love failure. And I am an expert at it.

I fail every single day. Sometimes I do it more than once, which makes me even happier.

So you're probably asking yourself, has DrJ slipped a gear or what?

Nope. You're getting, as they say on Twitter, #TRUTH.

Because if you are not failing, you are not trying hard enough.

Or, as the more poetic Robert Browning, suitor of the elusive Elizabeth Barrett, wrote: "Ah, but a man's reach should exceed his grasp, Or what's a heaven for?" And, as I hope you remember from high school English class, he did marry her despite parental interference, and apparently the result was quite heavenly.

So, what's your excuse for not failing?

In an informal survey I just did, I found that the reasons for not failing fall into three bins.

Some people just don't see their failures. Or shortcomings. Or reality, in its many shapes and forms. It's not a bad strategy, but in the long run, it makes for a lonely life. Sharing our frailties is a great way to make friends. What better gift to give someone than the freedom to be who they are, warts and all, and to know that you'll still want to hang out with them?

Then there are those who just don't attempt anything at all. They clock in and clock out and try not to do very much other than maybe drink coffee and grouse about office politics or the weather or any of the million other things over which they have no control. Maybe if they attempted something and failed at it, and repeated the cycle a few times, eventually they'd figure out how to actually get it done.

And then there are those who never bite off more than they can chew. And swallow. And digest. (I don't know how they figure that out, but maybe it's genetics, like curly hair or funny shaped toes.) People who are like this often have the most pristine resumes, the kind that HR managers love because they show 'progressive levels of responsibility.' You don't want to mess that sort of record up with multiply-pivoted startup experiences or a sabbatical spent building yurts in Oregon.

My main reason for wanting to fail is that I'm an entrepreneur. I always bite off way more than I can chew. (I used to have curly hair, but my toes are pretty normal, as were my parents, so I really don't know where that came from.) And I'm pretty lucky, because I get to work every day with a similar bunch of failure-lovers.

We're OK with failing in the short run, because the heaven we're reaching for is really, really far from our grasp. And we'll not be satisfied by just lowering the crossbar on the goalpost. In fact, we'd like to move it even higher. After all, the satisfaction is in the striving, as much as in the goal.

When your appetite for risk keeps you on the edge, it's easy to flip from failure to success!

@DrJanice: The school of hard knocks still grants the most valuable degree. #truth

It's easy to think that the more difficult the problem, the more you need an expert with lots of letters after their name. But really, the thorniest of life's problems often have the simplest of answers. You just have to ask the right person.

The Falconi Test

You may be quite adept at metrics, measurements, and even arcane bits of securities law, but if you're in manufacturing and haven't used the Falconi Test, read on.

A few years back, I got a call from Ken Krauss, who was then VP of Operations for US Axle, a very cool manufacturing company about an hour outside Philadelphia. (He's President now, so you know he's great at what he does, enough to meet the very high standards of the guy who hired him.) They use Teamability® because it predicts how people will work on a team, but he was calling to ask if I knew of anything useful for measuring engineering skills.

It turns out that some people tend to be better judges of their own abilities, and are less likely to cover up for their shortcomings. (In fact, many people revel in the things they do badly and are happy to tell you, for instance, how they can never find anything on their desk.) So this is a good start.

But Ken wanted an answer to the engineering question. And I had one, pulled from the annals of my past life in manufacturing, as president of a sheet metal shop.

There was another president of another sheet metal manufacturing company, and he was the most brilliant test developer I have ever met. He didn't have a PhD. I am pretty sure that it took his mother's prodding (and that of a few nuns highly skilled in student management) for him to graduate from high school, but I doubt he was ever interested in a career in research. He just understood people and he was a very clever entrepreneur. He never patented his test. He didn't name it either. So, although Frank is probably now manufacturing halo holders for angels, I am going to name it after him: The Falconi Test.

The Falconi Test has one simple piece of equipment: a steel rule with the first inch cut off and precisely finished to match the other edges. The result is a rule that starts at the one-inch mark instead of zero. Frank would give it to a job applicant and say something like, "mark off 3 5/16 inches on that paper." As you can well guess, there were many who simply looked at the 3, then counted 5 little hashes and made their mark. And, of course, they were wrong.

Engineers need to be precise, but they also have to (as it was said in the old days) 'keep their wits about them.' If they don't, then inconsistencies and inaccuracies can wreak all kinds of havoc, from wasted material and damaged machinery on up to dangerous flaws that result in very visible, very expensive, and even very dangerous failings – like the ones currently costing a maker of auto safety airbags a few billion dollars or so.

And of course, engineers also need to be team players. So now Ken can have it all.

It's a good feeling to have a satisfied customer and to honor an old friend at the same time.

@DrJanice: If you can think of 10 people who'd want to do business with you, you've got entrepreneurial potential.

Baseball is about teaming. Selling is about teaming. Really, everything in life that's good depends on your ability to team with others to get it.

Build It and They Will Team

Here in the very active Philly startup community, the boys (and girls) of summer are out on their fields of dreams, ripe with the belief that if they build a business, customers will follow.

What will they build?

They'll be building the physical infrastructure - even if the initial effort only occupies a bedroom or garage. And they'll likely be working on their IT infrastructure, perhaps using VOIP to integrate it with their telecommunications infrastructure, starting with laptops and mobile phones. If the plan is to manufacture something, they might be deeply into their supply chain or transportation infrastructures, and if they're in a more unusual field of endeavor, a specialized security or financial infrastructure might be in the works.

In almost every kind of operation, infrastructure issues are mission-critical. Any failure to ensure smoothly functioning interaction between infrastructure components will cost excess time and money, and may diminish the possibility of survival.

So how's your human infrastructure?

Now more than ever, people serve complex, interactive, mission-critical functions in business processes. Decades of economic and technological change have made it necessary for people to work together in ways that are less and less like industrial revolution foot soldiers, and more and more like an infrastructure. So no matter whether you start with two, or ten, or twenty people, you need the ones who can maintain the smoothly functioning interaction that is the essence of a successful business today.

In a manufacturing or supply infrastructure, lack of synchronization causes 'choke points' and in a telecommunications infrastructure, low quality or flawed components cause 'noise' and 'interference.' The same kinds of things happen when people don't connect, communicate, and coordinate with others. And, just as in other forms of infrastructure, a very small failure at a key juncture can cascade into major problems. That's why, in the 21st century, how well people team is bound to become as important as how much they know and what they've done.

If you want to build a successful business, focus on creating a high-quality, coherent human infrastructure.

Consider these factors in your plan:

- *Different people have different ways of serving team needs.* Make sure you aren't setting up the division of labor with a rigidly defined set of functional rules. You want team players, not robots, so recognize the fact that once you bring good people together, they will be able to work out a lot of the details without you. Stop thinking about job titles and, instead, organize each individual's job responsibilities to be consistent with their teaming qualities.

- *Wait till the team has practiced together – a lot – before attempting a big play.* People need a chance to discover their own orientation to working with others to solve problems and achieve group objectives. This could require a lot of low-risk practice time – although there are ways to speed it up. Teamability® comes to mind, for obvious reasons. But even so, you should create opportunities for your human infrastructure to 'jell' before you try playing on a bigger field, such as presenting to investors or going after a contract that is at the limit of the firm's proven capabilities.

- **_Don't forget to share the magic._** There is something magical about any entrepreneur's 'field of dreams': something that some dreamers may be tempted to hold back. It's not the same as the mission or the intellectual property. It's more like the reason behind the dream, like the true identity of the 'they' in 'if you build it, they will come.' Think about how to share your dream and how to keep it alive. It is a subtle source of power that will not only strengthen the existing human infrastructure, but will also attract exactly the kinds of people who recognize an opportunity to play a fulfilling position on your team!

@DrJanice: My personal Twitter #brand seems to be, 'umm did she really say that?'

It can be a lot of fun to write about things you think you know nothing about. It forces you to reach out to people who do know a lot – but only the ones who are willing to share it with you. In fact, I'm not sure which is more fun – the learning or the teaming!

Branding Yourself – without the pain in the...

Okay, so I have to start by admitting that when I first heard the term 'brand yourself' I thought of baby cows. As in, baby cows receiving the very painful and permanent imprint of someone's logo on their butts.

That image went away when I started hanging out with real branding experts. Corporate branding, I mean, where no animals are harmed in the making of the marks.

These people are really interesting, because you can dish about the stuff you buy, and they can tell you why you're buying it. (Sometimes, of course, an incredibly soft pair of black leather riding boots are just for keeping your legs warm and your feet dry in winter...while looking sensational with the bag you scored in an online sale, and the fact that both are from Cole Haan is just a coincidence. But I digress.)

We live in a blizzard of branding, so it was a surprise to hear from my friends Dr. Natalie Petouhoff and Laura Walton that brands are having a hard time these days. Apparently it's becoming increasingly difficult for them to deliver on their brand promises.

One thing I've known for a very long time is that delivering on promises is pretty important. I hadn't given much thought to making promises via an abstract intermediary, but, as Dr. Natalie and Laura pointed out, brands are very much like people, in the way that companies are sort of like people…in the legal sense. So it follows: sometimes companies make promises, and if the promises aren't kept, trouble ensues. Often, that kind of wrangling happens in a back room – or a courtroom. But when a brand makes (or carries with it) a promise, and doesn't keep it, the whole mess can happen right out in front of everybody, via Twitter, on Facebook, in the blogosphere, and in the media.

Now, having been raised to a new level of branding-awareness, I asked the esteemed legal advisor and intellectual property expert, Fred Wilf about promises. (Fred, by the way, is the guy who put the ® in Teamability®, for which we love him forever. And although he's an attorney, he speaks in a way that the rest of us who aren't can readily understand.)

So saith Fred, "In the legal context, a promise is a statement or declaration of intent. It can be written or oral. A written promise can be signed or unsigned. It can be unilateral or bilateral/multilateral (mutual). It can be made in exchange for something of value or the promise of payment of something of value ('consideration'). It can be made in exchange for another promise that does not include payment. Under the law, whether a promise becomes an enforceable contract depends on each of these facts, and a few more."

And as it often happens, Fred got me thinking about things I hadn't been thinking about, *to wit, **what if all brand promises had to meet the legal standard? What if my brand – what I promise you – was an enforceable contract?***

For any one of you who have taken the widely recommended advice to upgrade your image to a brand, I just want you to know one thing: Your brand promise may be the most important promise you ever make – and keep.

Keeping your brand promise isn't just a directive, a script, or a process. It's more like a world-view. You need some way of building and sustaining a living model of what you are and what you stand for. For organizations, that's usually called culture, but for a brand – or a person with a brand – there just isn't enough time to get something that big into a small package. Business or person, there's only one of you – and nothing to hide behind.

Your brand – and your brand promise – will stand or fall based on credibility. And despite all those assurances of privacy and confidentiality made by top-level-friends-and-followers-only infochannels, this is a social media world. There are no secrets.

So yes, dear reader, whether you're maintaining a company or a personal brand, you must maintain currency in keeping your promises, because people are watching and deciding all the time. Including me…and Fred.

Here's some basic advice:

First, make sure you know what you're promising.

I'm going to be blunt here. If you borrowed the concept for your brand promise from someone's website whose product is 'pretty similar' to yours, you blew it before you even got out of the gate. Promises – at least the good ones – arise from the heart and survive through integrity. (Perhaps you are old enough to remember the inherently equivocating "Promise her anything, but give her Arpége" advertising campaign. If so, you'll understand why it drove me to use any perfume BUT that brand.)

Second, make sure you are promising the right promise: the one your potential customer really wants.

Begin by drafting your promise; then reflect on it, and then air it out through your preferred channels. Are you promising a starry night where the earth moves? Something that ends happily ever after? Or is it just your 'thing' that's helpful and reliable? Before you set the promise in stone, you had better be sure of its connection – and its connotation. Remember DrJ's 5M rule: Mixed Messages Mostly Make Messes.

Finally, figure out how you're going to convince your potential 'consumer' that you really will be keeping your promise.

These days, few people take time to read all the copy. It's your brand that gets you up close and personal, and it's in that very tight space that the truth comes out. Not just with your followers and not just with your Facebook friends, but with everyone.

Adopt a platform of respect, appreciation, and gratitude – and make sure that the people on your team treat each other that way. If your brand gets mixed up in any one or more of the fifty shades of miserable management, you'll soon be sporting a danger sign that glows in the dark.

Brand credibility is something you have to earn on the shop floor, in the board room, in the middle of the late-night scrum session, in every conversation, every text, and every face-to-face, every day.

No matter how hard we try to connect with our customer, if we can't first connect with each other, then no brand – personal or otherwise – will ever rise to the standard of being a promise.

@DrJanice: Do you take better care of your car than yourself? #justasking

I'm not much of a car person, having grown up in New York City where there's a cab on every corner just waiting to drive you. (Well, maybe that's a Lyft or something like that now, but you get my drift. And the buses and subways were fine when I was a kid.) But a lot of you are with car. And I bet you do all those things they tell you to in that manual that must be somewhere in the glovebox or trunk or under the front seat. And you do them on time too, right? Ok then. Are you taking care of yourself as well?

The Seven Point Career Vehicle Check-Up

You can tell that summer is really underway when you get emails from auto repair shops promoting the Seven Point Summer Check-Up. I try to remember to take the old buggy in before June, because there's nothing worse than heading out in 90-degree heat, only to discover that the air conditioner is blowing hot air. But it's usually July before I get around to it, and by then I'm competing with everyone else whose car-care planning leaves a lot to be desired.

I used to have a T-shirt that proclaimed, "I may not be perfect, but parts of me are excellent!" (Props to Ashleigh Brilliant, the – ahem – brilliant author of that line.) It's true. I'm lacking the motor-driven vehicles part, but I'm pretty good at career vehicles (aka, 'jobs'). So while I can't help you with your car this summer, I can help you tune up your current position.

Here is a Seven-Point series of questions. If you can answer all of them with a resounding YES, you'll be able to stay cool and get where you want to go. If not, you might consider taking a peek into your owner's manual.

1. I am aware of the vision, mission, and/or goal for everything I do at work.

2. When problems arise — of any kind — they are usually resolved in a reasonable and efficient way.

3. My job responsibilities make sense to me, in terms of what my organization really needs.

4. I get respect and recognition from others in a manner that is meaningful to me.

5. My manager 'gets' me – consistently listens to me, values me, and encourages me to grow.

6. My coworkers feel like a real team to me – we share the load, we support each other, we have fun together, and we get the job done.

7. I may not have big-picture responsibility or an executive title, but I know that I make a significant contribution.

So, are you cruising along to your destination with cool confidence, or are you off-course, negotiating detours of frustration and dissatisfaction?

If the score on your check-up was less than what you consider optimal, here are some tips:

- First, to quote Socrates, Know Thyself. (Actually, being Greek, he probably said γνῶθι σαὑτόν.) But in any language, it's the best starting point from which to discover who you really want to be, and what sort of team contributions are really meaningful to you. If you're not too sure about these things, ask people who know and love you for their perspective on the kinds of activities that always seem to get you going and make you happy.

- Second, learn something new every day. You don't have to take a formal class to learn, and that's not necessarily the best way, either. Try connecting with someone who knows more about the topic than you do. It's called social learning, and it's a powerful force for developing your teamwork skills because you learn *with* other people.

- And last, read the seven points again and ask yourself this question: 'If I were in charge, how would I go about making each of these points universally true?' Then, pick a career destination where you believe it can happen.

Remember, the purpose of an automotive check-up is to keep the car in top condition so it can perform with excellence over the long haul. Doesn't your career deserve at least an equal level of care?

@DrJanice: Team on the job, team on a date. Basic skills are similar. #teamof2

Apparently, an apocalypse doesn't require zombies any more. And, apparently, all it may take to bring humanity down in mass reproductive failure is an app. A frustrating, yet addicting, app. But like many things in the digital world, there is a cure – in the real world. And all it takes is a swipe in the right direction.

Don't Swipe Left on Life

I followed a link on Tech Crunch and ended up on a site called The Dating Apocalypse. Never one to eschew news about future disasters, I clicked through a few places and saw some truly scary research findings, or at least reports of them. Since I haven't formally reviewed how people came to their conclusions, I'm just going to report a few items here and assume their numbers are acceptable. Then I'll pontificate.

- Fewer than one in ten men message someone they presumably 'won' a match from, and…

- More than half of communications – from people who swiped the same way you did – are ignored, so…

- One in 500 swipes, presumably in the right direction, gets you one exchange of phone numbers…

Oh dear. I'm not going to consider intervening variables for the moment. Let's stay on the big picture.

- 30% go on a date and expect it won't work out

Maybe you don't believe that expectations control outcomes but consider this:

- 90% swipe when bored

Back in the day, when one of my job titles was 'mother of

teenagers,' my daughter complained she was bored. And was promptly told – in stereo – that only boring people got bored. The rest of us found something interesting to do, or someplace else to go where – wonder of wonders, we might meet (or at least witness) other people who are doing things.

So it's bad enough to be trying to socialize when it's just you and an app and some words and pictures. Is it any wonder that (the researchers found) swiping is increasing most users' feelings of loneliness; more of them are expecting their messages to be ignored; there's a lot of lying, cheating, and damage to self worth; and there's apparently a lot of 'catfishing' and 'ghosting.'

Ok, maybe that's a plus. I learned new meanings for two words I thought I knew. But I'm not going to depress you by defining them, assuming you are likewise naïve about the new digital methods of romantic torture.

Dating apps are a lot like slot machines. You pay – in time or money – to try for a jackpot. And you know the odds are against you. But like a rat in a Skinner box, you keep your paws moving in a futile cycle of illusion that you have some power in a system designed to remove it from you.

So, what have we learned? (I mean other than that the makers of Hinge are upping their game by moving away from… the game.)

Swiping left is definitely not the way to happiness. And, likely, neither is swiping right, but at least it gives you a chance.

The problem is, it might not be a chance on what you either want or need. And, this is pretty much universal, no matter what we are talking about: romance, career, friendship, and everything in between. Because all of them are – or should involve – consensual acts between consenting adults.

Herewith, an approach that will help you maximize your win while minimizing your loss. Because this is your life we are talking about and I don't want you swiping left on it and giving up.

First, figure out what you want.

Then, figure out what you really need.

The second will likely look like a scaled-back version of the first. If they look pretty much the same, try to figure out how you are 'cheating' yourself. Because we can all want the moon but really, unless you love green cheese and hate gravity, it's not going to have as good a potential outcome as sharing a cheesesteak* with someone you're actually enjoying being with.

Take chances – because a life well-lived is full of chances taken. And most of those chances will never present themselves. You have to look for them.

And here is the most important part.

Swipe the things that *don't* work to get you what you really need – firmly and resolutely to the left.

And inevitably, you'll be swiping right on life.

* Cheesesteak may only apply if you are a native Philadelphian (which I am not) or an enthusiastic convert. Please feel free to substitute your regional favorite. For instance, if you are from Detroit, Better Made chips and a bottle of Faygo. Or, if Canadian, go with poutine. (Meaghan, our Canadian-born and bred Client Services Manager, just enlightened me.)

@DrJanice: Warning: Attainable goals may be damaging to your organization's efforts at #innovation.

While I don't like to get down in the details, I am pretty organized when the task at hand is visionary and requires a modicum of process. But then my desire to change the world kicks in and I start thinking, 'what would happen if…' And, inevitably, there's a revelation. And then I have to sell it to the rest of the team.

Being SMART may not be so smart after all.

Did you make any New Year's resolutions this year? If so, I'm guessing that some of them are still in the works, such as those involving goals for the 12 months ahead. Are they making you frustrated? It's no secret that, along with performance evaluations, goal setting is one of those things people never quite learn to love. And yet, setting goals is one of those things everyone (particularly authors and bloggers) expects successful business people to do, despite the fact that successful business people often hate doing things other people expect of them.

But tradition is tradition, so on January 1, I sat down, pen in hand, to jot some notes. And all I could think of was the old organizational command to make your plans **SMART**: **S**pecific, **M**easurable, **A**ttainable, **R**elevant, **T**ime-bound. Back in the day, these were supposed to be the delimiters of sure-fire goal setting. If your goal couldn't stand up to those, it just wasn't making the grade.

But this is now, and now is the age of innovation. And, being a lover (and creator) of innovation, I asked myself whether I should still be following the processes of an earlier era. Here's what emerged…

Specific stayed, because if a goal isn't specific, how do you ever figure out where you're headed?

And I kept *Measurable*, because although I don't like rating systems, I do like to have some idea of how far I've come, and whether I'm still on track.

Relevant made me think hard. When you have a very broad range of applications, or you're trying something completely new, then relevance may not be known at all during the planning stage, and can only emerge from the process. (For the fashion-aware, consider the problem of 'orphan' accessories. I once had a fabulous, but useless, beaded belt that I kept around for ages. Then one day an ensemble appeared in my closet that just screamed for turquoise beads.) Sometimes a thing will make itself relevant just by chance, which is a reason for accepting a loose definition of the word.

Then there was *Time-bound*: a no-brainer because I was thinking 'goals for the coming year' rather than the next decade or millennium.

Which brought me back to *Attainable*. That, too, seemed obvious…until I did a quick check in an online dictionary and learned that *Attainable things are within your reach.*

'Within reach' suggests that you can get what you want without a whole lot of stretch or effort. Now, if you keep a scoreboard that you like to decorate with a lot of wins, put plenty of 'attainables' on your to-do list. But if innovation and change are what you seek, then SMART goals need a warning label: *DANGER: Attainable goals may be damaging to your organization's ability to innovate.*

Focusing on attainable goals could also be a turn-off to the very people who are most capable of handling risk, making discoveries, and causing innovation! Those are the people who rarely ask if something is possible or not. They just go for the gold – asking bigger questions, covering more ground, trying harder, and stretching further.

In Lewis Carroll's 'Alice' books, there was the White Queen who said, "Sometimes I've believed as many as six impossible things before breakfast!" No one would accuse her of SMART planning – and yet, believing the impossible to be possible is a sure way to bypass the barrier of attainability. Can you imagine what might happen if your goals didn't need to be attainable? I can.

1. You'd have nothing to lose. With no one expecting sure-fire success, you could feel free to take some wild-ass swings. Sure, some will be whiffs, but you might just knock the ball out of the park. (Believe it or not, fear is the biggest cause of failure.)

2. You can still go for simple solutions. If they don't work, you'll be right: your goal wasn't attainable. But you'd be primed to succeed, so you'd try an alternative path. And another, and another. And should you eventually get there, so much the better! (Being right and winning are not the same – but they're not mutually exclusive.)

3. You'd forever leave the ranks of the narrow-minded; the people who put the 'no' in innovation, joining instead the ones who bring positive change and brighter futures.

May your 'impossible' of this year become your successful achievement of the next!

@DrJanice: Be good at what you are good at. Nothing else makes sense. #career

In the spirit of public service to those hardy souls going through extended interview processes, I agreed to speak to a writer. And while I was supposed to be giving her my expertise so she could make her living, I actually learned something that's served mine for a very long time.

Timing Isn't Everything

Many years ago, I was interviewed about personality tests. Specifically, I was asked how someone could 'pass' one. The writer, Gail Harlow, had been through many in her life as an employee, and could never figure out what she was doing 'right' or 'wrong.' This left her quite frustrated because she was naturally curious and had a streak of logical thought that made her ask the most interesting questions.

So, over coffee – three cups as I recall – I gave Gail some history of personality tests and told her where we were going with current research that was not about personality (and which eventually formed the foundation of Teamability®). She was fascinated but her assignment was to help her readers with some tips and tricks. And, of course, she had a deadline. I remember her saying so clearly how important timing would be. At the moment, of course, I assumed she was talking about her own deadline. Because when you're inventing something as new as Teamability, you really can't think about timing because it's just so long between idea and launch.

Luckily, I saved a copy of her article so I can now quote myself. Apparently, one thing I said was, "try to avoid committing to strong words like always and never." If we were still talking now (in which case, I would be up to coffee #15,758) I would hope I'd remember to add, "and words like nothing and everything."

34

There are a few words in the English language as powerful as those. They are absolutes. And while I'm personally fine with some absolutes, especially the ones that start "Thou shalt not," I wouldn't necessarily hold other people to the same standards.

That's the problem with absolutes. There's no wiggle room.

So when I'd hear people tell me – in many contexts – that timing is everything, I'd naturally feel uncomfortably constrained. Choked sometimes. Because I knew that I personally possessed virtually no sense of timing in the clock sense of time. Some days I'd work very long hours and it seemed like minutes. Other times, I'd seem to be working in my sleep. I'd just wake up and there would be paper with my less-than-neat handwriting on it, full of a new plan or bit of tech solution.

Some things don't fit, even when they seem like they should. (Oh yes, 'should.' Another word that's short on wiggle room.)

And then one day, it all fell it place. Maybe the timing was just right. I don't know. I forgot to wind the watch, or maybe I never had one.

I no longer had to worry about the clock, because there was someone else who was an expert in that. And, because Mark Talaba – TGI's Vision Former – and I were on to the same big vision, which was timeless for me (in the clock-time sense,) it was easy to turn the timing-that-is-everything over to him.

As for me, I kept to the big picture, timing-is-forever version that I live best in. But I learned what I didn't do well or like very much.

What happened after that was sort of funny. It turned out that the reason my 'good timing' partner understood my 'bad timing' self was that he really could do both kinds of timing. He was just better than me at crossing the 'time line!'

So when the opportunity to do a TEDx talk came around, he insisted I get a real coach, one who would make sure I would actually do my allotted minutes in real-time minutes, not DrJ minutes (which can vary from 5 seconds to 20 months, apparently.)

So Laura Walton did the timing. Which I hated. But which I did anyway. And which I eventually learned to love.

Because it turned out that Laura and I were teaming well. Just as I had been doing with Gail, and later, Mark.

You can see the resulting video here: http://bit.ly/DrJaniceTED

@DrJanice: Team Chemistry is just a matter of the right elements, the right catalyst & just enough heat to get cooking!

Part 2: Teaming

Were it not for the most fundamental act of teaming, there would be no human race — or birds, or reptiles, or insects, or even most plant life. And really, why would anyone want to hang around with a bunch of bacteria, fungi, and single-cells anyway? Boring!

No wonder so many people have found so many different ways to express wonderment and appreciation for all of what teaming brings to life!

"It's not just about whether you can compete with your peers... It's also about whether you can come together and work together with them to make our world stronger."
— *Michelle Obama*

"Great things in business are never done by one person, they're done by a team of people."
— *Steve Jobs*

"Find a group of people who challenge and inspire you, spend a lot of time with them, and it will change your life."
— *Amy Poehler*

"Individual commitment to a group effort is what makes a team work, a company work, a society work, a civilization work."
— *Vince Lombardi*

"Not me. Us."
— *Senator Bernie Sanders*

"A group is a bunch of people in an elevator. A team is also a bunch of people in an elevator, but the elevator is broken!"
— *Bonnie Edelstein*

"I can do things you cannot. You can do things I cannot. Together we can do great things."
— *Mother Teresa*

"No member of a crew is praised for the rugged individuality of his rowing."
— *Ralph Waldo Emerson*

"How could you have a soccer team if all were goalkeepers? How would it be an orchestra if all were French horns?"
— *Desmond Tutu*

"Teamwork is the ability to work as a group toward a common vision, even if that vision becomes extremely blurry."
— *Author Unknown*

"None of us is as smart as all of us."
— *Ken Blanchard*

"When 'I' is replaced by 'We,' illness becomes wellness."
— *Shannon L. Alder*

@DrJanice: On our #Team everyone is a star. And they're in the same constellation. #futureofwork

Teamwork is present wherever people join together to achieve a common goal. But the pursuit in which the need for teaming is most obvious and ever-present is in team sports. After all, TEAM is right there in the name! A one-to-one relationship might be called a marriage; add a few more people and it might be called a community group, a club, or a congregation; a business could be called a store, or a department, or a division. But in sports, both the players and their organizations are known as teams. And, of course, they all have the rules by which they play.

The Ground Rules

Every sport has Ground Rules, which the dictionary defines as "...rules pertaining to the limits of play on a particular field." For instance, in baseball, a batter can blast a pitched ball right out of the park, but if it's on the wrong side of either foul pole, it's not a home run and the distance counts for nothing.

Well, it turns out that teamwork itself has ground rules, and when they are understood, it becomes a lot easier to know what really counts, and what doesn't.

The foundational concepts of Teamability® didn't come from psychology, but rather, from physics and systems theory. That's because teaming doesn't just happen in the mind, but also in physical reality, where ground rules apply. And the field that we play in is represented by a unified field theory of how people operate in the world. That's what I'll try to explain here.

'Team' is often described as a group of people who have been brought together to achieve a goal. Of course, this is true in the sense of Person-to-Person (P2P) teamwork, where people form on-the-job relationships. It works, just like many things we do in our ordinary lives. But it's primarily transactional.

Team Members: P2P
} Interactions & Relationships

© The Gabriel Institute

There is an important qualitative difference between people working side by side, and a group of people who feel a sense of common purpose and meaning in support of something greater than themselves.

Teaming: P2T
} Mutual Awareness, Respect, and Trust. Shared commitment to something larger than 'self' or 'other.'

© The Gabriel Institute

Person-to-Team (P2T) teaming is akin to what most people call 'team chemistry' or 'team spirit.' It springs from a powerful connection between individuals and the team itself, as a living entity, and is the basis for consistently positive, supportive relationships between teammates. The results: positive engagement, intense commitment, and extraordinary – even transformational - individual and team achievement.

The Elements of Teaming

Having recognized the importance of a Team having a life of its own, and needs of its own, the creators of Teamability made the leap from the traditional focus on individual traits, skills, and talents, to a holistic and integrative focus on the ways different people seek to serve team needs. This 'operating system of teamwork' is directly modeled and addressed by Teamability technology and its integrated management methods.

When we began to consider the Team as a living, breathing organism – one that envelops and responds to the people who serve it – the questions that first came to mind were 'What does the team need to ensure its livelihood?' and 'Do different people seek to serve specific team needs?' The answers were straightforward – although it took a long time to prove them out. Ultimately, we came to the conclusion that all organizations – no matter how large or small – had the same set of needs, and that the Teams that make up an organization are typically comprised of sub-sets of these ten needs. We also validated the theory that a person's orientation to serving a specific team need could be identified and qualified.

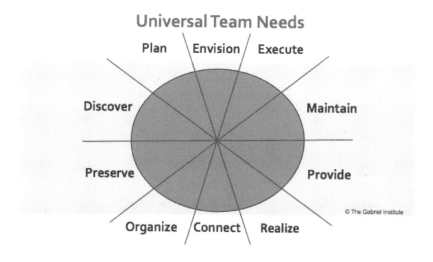

The Teamability Roles

In the language of Teamability, the term 'Role' identifies a person's sense of connection to one or more of the universal Team needs.

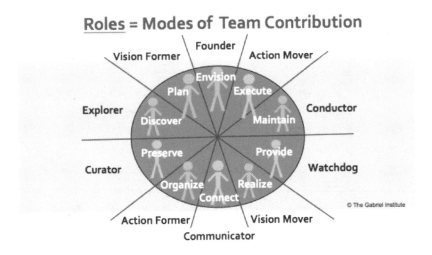

Roles = Modes of Team Contribution

© The Gabriel Institute

Role is important on every level of organizational functioning:

- For the individual, it expresses the most prominent mode of contribution. People who have a well-developed Role feel driven to give to something larger than themselves. Many people experience their Role as their 'mission in life.'

- For the team, Roles enable the distribution of job responsibilities to people who will do them well – and will enjoy doing them. This makes it possible to align the Roles on a team with the mission of the team.

- For the organization, awareness of Role is the fundamental way of understanding, improving, and capitalizing on the strengths of a human infrastructure: the synergetic value and maximization of team chemistry, which is reflected in bottom-line performance.

Some people have developed more than one Role, and Roles can have modifying aspects that further inform team leadership, decision-making, and collaboration.

Coherence

Coherence applies to all Roles, although it does not have the same degree of significance in all situations. That's because teamwork – even positive, productive teamwork – comes with components of stress and ambiguity.

People who team in a coherent manner accept, and even welcome, the challenges of team interaction and achievement. They may even prefer to add new challenges and responsibilities as they go. There is a technical term for stress that we enjoy: *eustress*. It is beneficial and healthy, whether we are scaling a mountainside, facing an adversary in a negotiation, or engaging in business in an uncertain environment.

Diffuse ← Coherent → Rigid

© The Gabriel Institute

Coherent teaming is *not* about competence.
It addresses stress response, workplace fit, and related issues.

People who are not generally tolerant of stress will typically have one of two alternate reactions to it. On one side, they may team in a rigid manner, tending to focus on small details when they would be better off taking in the big picture. Under stress, rigid teaming can lead to contentious interaction and resistance to change, sometimes without adequate and timely consideration of potential adverse effects. When this happens, it can result in problems with people, productivity, service delivery, and in the creative atmosphere that is essential to innovation.

On the opposite side of the coin is diffuse teaming under stress. People who respond to workplace challenges in this way tend to dissipate, rather than focus, their energy. They may be overly concerned with being diplomatic, or simply with 'blending in.' Unfortunately, these responses often reduce positive team contribution, even when a person has the appropriate knowledge and skills and sincerely wishes to use them.

Understanding coherence plays an important part in helping people and teams succeed. It facilitates constructive interaction with team members, and better matching of people to work assignments and business situations.

Teaming Characteristics

Teaming Characteristics (TCs) describe specific qualities of a person's interactions with others, both inside and outside the team. TCs are neither good nor bad on their own, but are only significant within a situational context.

For example, consider the TC indicating that a person is 'not an up-close manager,' which might seem negative at first glance. However, this teaming characteristic can also be very positive.

First, think of an executive leader with a high-powered team of seasoned professionals. Managing such a team in an 'up-close' manner could be seen as micro-management, or intimidation, or worse. Now consider a very different business context: a supervisor in a call center. Here, managing less experienced, lower paid workers in a high-turnover field *requires* up-close management. So the successful manager in the former situation might be a terrible fit in the latter – and vice versa.

Analyzing the required interactions of a particular position will reveal the likely relevance and impact of a particular Teaming Characteristic.

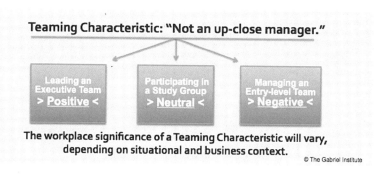

Teaming Characteristic: "Not an up-close manager."

| Leading an Executive Team > Positive < | Participating in a Study Group > Neutral < | Managing an Entry-level Team > Negative < |

The workplace significance of a Teaming Characteristic will vary, depending on situational and business context.

© The Gabriel Institute

Note that in many situations, a particular Teaming Characteristic can be mostly, or entirely, neutral. Other TCs could interfere with at least one critical success factor of a particular position.

The Elements of Team Operation

There are some logical principles that help management design effective, high performance teams, and distribute the work to the right team members. These integrated methods can be adopted and applied by the organization to stimulate engagement, energize collaboration, and generate positive team chemistry.

Role-fit: Most people will be at their best when their job responsibilities are aligned with their Role.

Need: Someone to ensure that the report is Perfect.

Don't ask a Founder

- Great with big-picture issues; not with small details
- Always sees a bright future
- Wants to inspire, not just inform

Ask a Conductor

- Pays close attention to immediate needs
- Enjoys finding and fixing errors
- Wants things to be done right!

Role-fit simplifies ad hoc decision-making
Less stress, more engagement, better results

© The Gabriel Institute

Team-fit: Most teams have a specific mission – a reason for being – and the challenges related to that mission will call for the capabilities associated with different Roles. Ultimately, people who have positive fit for both the job responsibilities and for the context of the work (the team's mission) are the people most likely to achieve and sustain high levels of performance.

Team-Fit: Mission Determines Essential Roles

There are occasional exceptions, but in general, team performance will be at its best when all of the essential Roles that the team needs to meet its mission are present, and there are no team members whose Role does not align in some way with the needs of that particular team.

Role-pairing: Each Role has a complementary Role Partner. When we identify these natural partnerships, whether or not both Roles fulfill immediate team needs, we design into the team a way to create and capitalize on human synergy.

Role-pairs Energize Each Other, and the Team

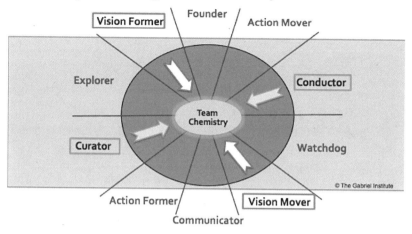

Role-respect: Blanket, generic expressions of appreciation and respect for colleagues are of limited value as motivators – and may even become damaging to team chemistry. The most effective way to deliver thanks or praise is to find a way to say something that aligns with the person's mode of contribution: their Role.

Role-keyed Messages Are More Meaningful

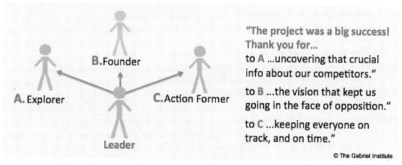

People experience words of appreciation or respect
according to their mode of team service.

New Forms of Leadership and Management Guidance

Implementing Teamability does not necessarily supplant familiar tools or methods. Rather, we have found that a better understanding of people's desire to do meaningful work builds upon existing processes and resident expertise.

Teamability's integrated set of distinctions for aligning people with job responsibilities, with team mission, and with situational and contextual conditions, invariably adds value for leaders, for team members, and for the organization, as well as for clients and stakeholders.

Teamability Reports describe the different ways that people intrinsically seek to make meaningful team contributions, including specific qualities of their teaming interactions. This information is invaluable in selecting, developing, managing, and motivating people to reach new heights of team contribution. In fact, a team – or an entire organization – can become more resilient, more collaborative, and more productive, simply by experiencing Teamability and using the self-coaching feedback.

Team Analysis Reports produce new forms of management information by depicting the collaborative structure of teams in terms of best-fit to job responsibilities, best-fit to serve the specific mission of the team, and overall orientation to positive, constructive teamwork. Each analysis includes concise advisories and specific action steps for raising both individual and team performance.

Teamability Playbooks for Leaders connect the Leader's own 'teaming specs' with those of each person on their team, based on information derived from Team Analysis and individual Teamability reports. Playbook content gives Leaders concise and effective direction for communicating with direct reports and/or key team members. Playbooks also provide in-depth understanding of each team member's interests and motivations, which in turn improves general management and team-building skills, while also reducing stress.*

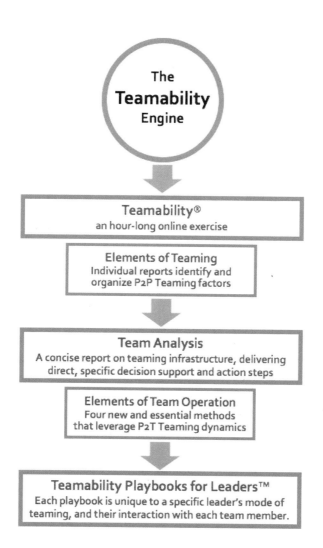

The Teamability Engine

Teamability®
an hour-long online exercise

Elements of Teaming
Individual reports identify and
organize P2P Teaming factors

Team Analysis
A concise report on teaming infrastructure, delivering
direct, specific decision support and action steps

Elements of Team Operation
Four new and essential methods
that leverage P2T Teaming dynamics

Teamability Playbooks for Leaders™
Each playbook is unique to a specific leader's mode of
teaming, and their interaction with each team member.

* *Teamability theories and practices have been extensively applied in real-world situations, and are producing an abundance of positive – even extraordinary – – business benefits. But teaming situations can be extremely complex, and are often subject to unexpected and/or uncontrollable outside influences. So, while our methods have proven to be effective and reliable in a wide range of applications, business outcomes and measurable value will vary from case to case.*

@DrJanice: I define #engagement as you bring your mind, heart, and soul to work every day. For some jobs, body optional.

An engaged employee is described, variously, as one who is fully involved in and enthusiastic about his or her work; who acts in a way that furthers the organization's interests; who will go the extra mile for colleagues and customers. Note: A portion of this article previously appeared in the 'Seven Point Career Vehicle Check-up,' regarding you and what you do. Here, it's in a teaming context.

Getting Engaged

Big city high-rises often have exercise/pool areas that rival the best-equipped health clubs. I like to use the one in my building as a study. Late one evening, relaxing in the hot tub after a day of constant business activity, I was joined by two young professionals who were having a discussion – actually a debate – on the topic of 'engagement' surveys. One is a psych major turned HR manager and the other a product manager with a degree in marketing. I'm going to call them 'Psych' and 'Product.'

Psych was asking Product if he could get her a copy of the Gallup Q12 – a set of questions that test for employee engagement, so she could use it to survey people in her company. Product pointed out that the Q12 is copyrighted material, and went on to lecture Psych about the value of such attitude surveys – or more accurately, the lack thereof. He must have taken great notes in class. He cited chapter and verse from product marketing literature, summing it up by stating categorically that although people might give you rave reviews, if they aren't buying your product, who cares?

Psych was not convinced. She had been given an assignment by her boss, and was determined to follow through. I felt sorry for her.

If you are – or know – someone who feels compelled to measure engagement, especially if the assignment has career-altering consequences, here's a set of questions that you can offer without exposing them to copyright infringement litigation. Why am I doing this? Well, I've done 30 years of study and research on what makes great teams great, and I know there is a big difference between a person's attitude about their place on a team (their level of engagement, if you will) and the underlying factors that influence 'teaming' behavior. The former will tell you about existing conditions. The latter will tell you why, and what you can do about it, thereby bridging the gap between attitudes and business results. (see www.teamability.com)

Here are my survey questions. Tell people to rank them on a scale from 1 (strongly disagree) to 5 (strongly agree). (If you want to credit me and send a link to your results, even better.)

The 'Teamability® 7':

1. I know the vision, purpose, and/or goal for everything I do at work.

2. When problems arise – of any kind – they are usually resolved in a reasonable and efficient way.

3. My job responsibilities are aligned with my desire to serve my team and my organization.

4. I get respect and recognition from others in a manner that is meaningful to me.

5. My manager 'gets' me – consistently listens to me, values me, and encourages me to grow.

6. My coworkers feel like a real team to me. We share the load, we support each other, we have fun together, and we get the job done.

7. I may not have the most important job in the company, but I know that I make a significant contribution.

I'm sure you know what you want, so I don't have to tell you the 'right' answers.

Oh, and just in case you are wondering what happened between the two young professionals in the hot tub…

I just heard they are getting engaged.

@DrJanice: Your company merged? Please welcome your new sibs and share your toys. #justsaying

Second marriages have a higher failure rate than first ones, and third marriages are even harder to succeed at. (Reported US numbers indicate that 50% of first, 67% of second, and 73% of third marriages fail. One can only shudder at the failure rates of those brave enough to try more than thrice.) So why is anyone surprised that corporate mergers fail?

For Better or Worse: The Post-Merger Challenge

Mergers are like marriages. They start off with the best of intentions and public proclamations of mutual respect, honor, and going forth to prosper and multiply. Champagne corks pop, and it feels like the honeymoon will last forever.

Then reality sets in.

In marriage, you consolidate two separate lives. In merger, you consolidate two separate living entities. If the union works, you end up with a winning team.

It's the 'if it works' part that troubles us, because we know the stats.

With such a high percentage of US marriages ending in divorce, you have to wonder why so many people press on to repeat the marriage/divorce/remarriage cycle. Sounds a little like some serial business-empire-builders, no? Hoping against hope that 'this time I'll get it right...'

The sad thing is, the success rate of business mergers comes in a distant second to that of marriages. Bain & Company (2004) put the U.S. failure rate at 70%, defined in terms of failure to increase shareholder value. Hay Group and the Sorbonne (2009) found that more than 90% of mergers in Europe fail to achieve their financial goals.

It looks like only one out of every ten champagne bottles is worth the pop. So much for pre-nups.

Let me put my behavioral scientist/marriage therapist hat on (yes, it is a big hat) to add some detail.

Failing marriages tend to follow a similar pattern. The dream of a happy ending carries people through the hills and valleys for a while, but eventually the underlying disjoints take their toll. It turns out that the once happy couple differs on how and when to communicate, what the mutual goals really are, and who is responsible for what. Stress levels mount, and when the stresses cannot be resolved, the union crumbles in a storm of blame and shame.

Post-merger, the structural challenges are vastly more complex, but the goals are essentially the same: keep the ball rolling; find efficient ways to redistribute resources, responsibility, and activity; and ensure that the members of the new team are on the same page, aligned with the goals of increasing baseline value and extending the lifespan of the organization. Doesn't that seem reasonable?

So whether we are talking about newly married couples or newly married teams, the general result we need to see is a positive impact that each side has on the other's environment. They grow in some meaningful way. The synergy of the couple may produce small human beings, or something purely cerebral or artistic. The synergy of an organization may produce social well-being, economic growth, and other benefits. To be successful, each kind of pairing must become a fully functioning team, coherently, effectively, and consistently producing value (including happiness, prosperity, community).

Now consider what really happens. Far too often, the post-merger scenario is chaotic. The people popping champagne corks envision new levels of growth, competitive advantage, and profitability, while the others are thrown into survival panic. Especially in times of economic uncertainty, fear of being downsized is contagious. Except for the few people whose future is actually written into the deal, even a place on the upside of the power curve is no guarantee of safety.

Executive leadership is focused on making changes to the operating, financial, and technology infrastructures, and wants the overhaul to be implemented on schedule. Nothing wrong with taking a logistical approach, but with few exceptions, the impact of change on the organization's _human_ infrastructure (execs included) is taken for granted. It is just assumed that people will somehow continue to team well together and carry on. That's why it's always a surprise when a merger fails to live up to expectations. Just like a marriage.

We already know that positive teamwork is essential to success, and that stress can dissipate, or even deactivate, team synergies. This leads us to two conditions that are missing from pre- and post-merger plans and activities. They are:

1) The recognition of team synergy as a mission-critical asset.

Viewing people as human resources, human capital, or talent suggests that they can be treated as interchangeable parts or units of cost, and that a powerful team can be created by matching up resumes, career paths, and skill sets. Sports teams provide some of the most obvious examples that this concept doesn't work reliably, but innumerable proofs also litter the history of business enterprise. (Remember that Enron was built on the principle of hiring 'only the best and brightest' and was celebrated as both a 'best place to work' and a 'most respected corporation'—before descending into chaos, bankruptcy, and criminal prosecution.)

But if we simply adopt the concept of people as 'human infrastructure' (vs. resources, capital, etc.) the importance of fostering and preserving _high-quality_ human interaction takes its rightful position as a strategic imperative.

2) Understanding and predicting the qualities with which people will work together to achieve common objectives.

Post-merger, the most reliable way to meet the forecasts for <u>business</u> performance is to have an effective way to forecast <u>human</u> performance.

Here are the teaming metrics you need to know about:

- **Role**: a person's affinity for one or more specific modes of service to the needs of a team

- **Coherence**: expressed as positive, flexible, constructive teaming behaviors under varying conditions of stress and ambiguity

- **Teaming Characteristics**: individual styles of responding and relating to others, subject to situational context

- **Role-fit**: an appropriate match between a person's Role and their assigned set of job responsibilities, raising individual performance and engagement

- **Team-fit**: structuring a team to include the Roles that are best fit to the team's mission, to optimize overall team performance

- **Role-pairing**: known, replicable synergies between specific Roles, which improve resilience and team chemistry

- **Role-respect**: the unique manner in which people of different Roles experience appreciation and respect, used in management to build trust and team stability

Whether you are considering a personal or a corporate merger, it's positive synergy you're after — not just a laundry list of common interests or competencies. Get the human infrastructure metrics right and the outcome really will be 'till death (not divorce or dissolution) us do part.'

@DrJanice: There's no little blue pill for startup failure. But there's hope. #Teamability

People don't like to talk about failure. It's not that they don't recognize that it happens — they do, but they just don't know why, and that's uncomfortable. But when you understand that failure is simply the team not being able to meet its mission because its needs aren't all being met, you <u>can</u> figure out what's missing. You might even be able to correct it in time.

Does Your Team Suffer From Connectile Dysfunction?

According to recent research by Shikhar Ghosh, a senior lecturer at Harvard Business School, data from more than 2,000 companies indicates that 75% of venture-backed startups fail.

Of course, there are different ways to define failure, but losing all the money you've put in — or losing your dream — certainly qualifies. Some might use shorter-term benchmarks, like achieving sales and revenue targets within a given timeframe, in which case an even higher percentage of funded startups would probably wind up sporting a big red F.

This is important, not just for startup teams and not just for investors, but for the U.S. economy as well. This chart showing 33 years of net annual job growth tells you why: Startup ventures create jobs. Big companies don't.

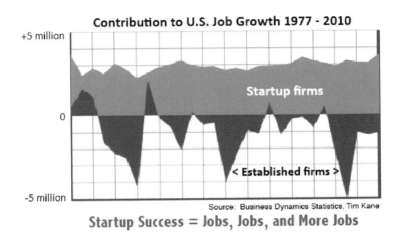

Contribution to U.S. Job Growth 1977 - 2010

Startup firms

< Established firms >

Source: Business Dynamics Statistics, Tim Kane

Startup Success = Jobs, Jobs, and More Jobs

So the really big questions are, why do so many startups fail and what can be done about it?

Studies have identified various issues that contribute to the collapse of startup teams, including competitive factors, market factors, and technology churn. But the #1 – by a long shot – indicator of pending demise can be summarized with just one diagnosis: Connectile Dysfunction.

CD, as we team-oriented entrepreneurs call it, causes the heartbreak of startup failure, which leads to chronically depressed economies.

Sound dangerous? Contagious? Fatal? It can be…but thankfully, CD is diagnosable and treatable. There's even a way to immunize against it.

CD happens when the way in which people connect with each other lacks sufficient respect, trust, and faith in the team vision. This can happen with people on the team, as well as with customers, investors, vendors, and the larger social community.

CD creates disappointment, misunderstandings, and stress. This exacerbates the problem, and also blocks quick resolution. The side effects can have long lasting, demoralizing effects on every team member.

So, let's say you believe your team has some level of CD and just isn't up for the challenge. (Yes, there is a spectrum of severity for this disorder.) What to do?

Start by asking these not-so-simple questions:

1. Do you have the right people on the team? That is,
    a. Do they actually want to do the work they are doing?
    b. Do they do the work at the quality level the job demands?
    c. Are they relatively free of ways of working together that you don't want to encourage in your culture?

2. Are they doing their work in a way that keeps their connections with people 'clean and clear'? Do they have the right kind of supports and do they have the appropriate level of autonomy?

3. Have you noticed any particularly odious qualities pertaining to the way they interact with others?

Keep in mind that 75% of VCs and private investors thought they knew the answers to these crucial teaming problems. But they didn't, and it cost them plenty. Now they are probably a little gun-shy and less likely to pull the trigger on the next startup opportunity, which won't do anything for the economy.

A variety of new approaches, from neurological studies to the mining of 'big data,' are being applied to the search for new ways to identify, assemble, and lead the right teams for the right mission. One such technology elicits 'teaming' behavior, and takes a direct measure of the different ways that individuals seek to contribute to organizational needs, thereby producing analytics of team chemistry, and new ways to structure and manage teams for optimal performance.

Now picture an island holiday, a glass of fine wine at sunset beneath swaying palms, with the promise of great things to come hanging heavy in the air: profit sharing, stock grants, market domination, all culminating in a climactic liquidity event.

That's reality for some entrepreneurs – the ones who built great teams. So before you invest your dreams, time, energy, and/or money, take personal responsibility for preventing CD, and look for help in the areas of team analysis, teaming analytics, and team development.

You could start by tweeting me, @DrJanice. *Stat!*

@DrJanice: Sometimes you just need a little extra to get them to sit up and notice you. #justsaying

Yes, this title is a little provocative. But you know, a girl has to do what she has to do. And sometimes the extra effort pays off with a big boost.

You're Leaning In. Have You Tried a Pushup?

No I'm not shilling for Sheryl Sandberg or Victoria's Secret here, although I've read one and worn the other. And I'm not talking about women vs. men, either.

What I'm talking about is your career, and I mean YOU, no matter what your DNA or externals say about your gender. Many of us are in the habit of playing down our assets, and while there are some good reasons for doing that, there also are some not-so-good reasons.

One, our assets – talents, skills, experience and other qualities – are so familiar to us. We use them every day, so it's hard to think of them as special. We assume that what we bring to the table, anyone can. And we're wrong.

Two, we rarely experience genuine appreciation for the ways in which we wholeheartedly contribute to the work of our teams. We may get donuts in the morning, pizza on Friday, or a pat on the back sometime in between, but research* has shown that different people experience respect and appreciation in very different ways. Unfortunately, most people express appreciation in a one-size-fits-all fashion. And they're wrong.

Three, in many work environments, everyone's expected to be tough and independent. Asking for, and even giving, too much help is thought to be weak. Sometimes, no matter how much we accomplish or what our colleagues or bosses may say about it, we don't feel that we've made a meaningful contribution.

This happens when we're good at what we do, but our job responsibilities are out of whack with who we really are. And everyone's wrong.

So let's hear it for the push up.

A push up happens when the inner you – your Role in service to a team – is being satisfied by the things you do.

It could be that you inspire people. Or you drive progress. You enlighten others and help them become their best selves. You lead the action. You manage the follow through. You have a knack for bringing valuable things back to the team, or making the most out of the limited resources your team has available. You fix the stuff that needs fixing. You preserve and organize and share knowledge that otherwise would be lost. You generate good feelings and build community. Each of these different kinds of contributions is central to a different Role. Whatever it is that you do because you love to do it, and keep doing because your organization needs it – that's your greatest asset.

Now take your greatest asset and make something more of it. It's as simple as one, two, three.

One, at the start of each day, remember that whatever you will be doing is more than a contribution to your colleagues or your customers. It's also a contribution to the world at large. Call it a ripple in a pond, a drop of water in the river of life, a stabilizing vibration in a chaotic universe, or whatever makes sense to you, but never lose sight of the fact that positive teaming makes a difference. If you don't make an effort each day to push up, then there's a good chance that you will experience a push down. (Don't confuse a push down with a put-down. Put-downs come from people who mistakenly assume that they will feel better if they make other people feel worse.)

Two, recognize and accept the fact that, for most people, showing appreciation is in the same category as politeness. Even when sincerely felt, it is usually expressed generically. It's very possible that you are 'secretly appreciated,' and you can help that secret come out of hiding. Which of your assets would you wish most to be recognized, and how best might that happen? Here's one approach: ask your manager for some feedback on the ways that your contributions add value to the team. You might say that you're trying to figure out how to be more valuable so you're trying to get a baseline. In an exchange like this, you'll find opportunities to raise awareness of your own particular teaming assets, even if your manager hasn't noticed.

Three, please remember that interdependency is the spice of life. It's common to say that 'timing is everything', but it's truer to say that '*teaming* is everything'. None of us is perfect and no one should be expected to do everything well. Even though some people CAN do just about anything well, that doesn't mean that they find the doing of it all to be meaningful or enjoyable. It's better for them, and for every member of a team, to share responsibilities and for each to do what makes them happy. And that happens best when you have each other to lean on – and help each other push up!

---

* A key finding of the research that led to the development of Teamability® showed that a person's mode of contributing to organizational need – their measurable 'Role' on a team – is closely aligned with the way in which they internalize expressions of respect that have been communicated by others.

@DrJanice: Stop thinking about your #leadership. Really. It belongs to your team.

People often ask me how to measure something abstract, like leadership, or innovation, or success, and then they fight me when I tell them they're asking the wrong question. So for one particular instance, I went ahead and wrote the test...and the scoring, which is really what was wanted even more than the questions. Now please, no more arguments. I can guarantee you'll be able to get the results you want.

Leadership Presence is More Than Just Being There

Now I'm not knocking charisma. It's useful and people tend to be attracted to it. And, from the leader's perspective, it can seem kind of easy. You just show up.

Problem is, that approach only works for well-established and/or highly visible guru-ninja-rockstar leaders. The rest of us need to do our homework before that big day arrives.

So here's your assignment. It's in three parts because, really, increasing your Leadership Presence involves complex, interrelated factors.

1. **Identify and clarify your vision of the future**, not only for yourself but for those you lead, or want to lead. Document your vision *(in writing!)* and then communicate it in a way that inspires people to follow it.

2. **Consider how you appear to others**. Start with your appearance, but give more than a passing glance at your inner self and soul (or whatever you call that intangible part of you that projects your values.) Do something to improve at least one of the above, every day.

3. **Get some practice in leaving decisions to other people**, especially to those who really want to contribute in the way that decision-making requires. *(This sounds easier than it is. People who want to lead generally like to be in control.)*

Finished already? OK! But before you try to send in your homework *(or send me a note saying your dog ate it)*, understand this: I am not going to grade you. You are going to do it, using your own standards. *(This is an old professorial strategy to discourage cheating, even though I know you weren't even thinking of doing that.)*

Here's how to score yourself, on a scale of 1 (low) to 5 (high):

Scoring Part 1 of your assignment is achieved by first calculating the number of your followers. You can do a headcount of people who report to you, or just use the number of followers on your Twitter or LinkedIn. Next, throw that number out, forget about it, and ask yourself this question: "What is the essence of my vision for the team, and how many of my followers know it, and are striving to achieve it?" *(This is a true measure of the enduring leader.)*

Your score on the second part is a little trickier. The fact is, some people rise to leadership positions purely because they focus their ambition on leadership *status*, rather than on leadership *effectiveness*. So the question is, how much of your quest for Leadership Presence is coming from your desire to serve your team, vs. buffing your image and/or padding your paycheck? Only *meaningful* change counts for this one. For example, it's an important part of your leadership presence to be a role model for self-improvement. *(However, to be clear, losing five pounds should not be scored as a five.)*

Your score on the third part requires a different kind of metric. Ask yourself how much of your leadership focus is applied to giving your team members the opportunity to make decisions. Then go ask them, one by one, if they feel you butted in on their decisions in any way. *(Look them in the eye when you ask this, and for leadership's sake, please smile!)*

You can put your score on a plaque for your office wall, if you like. Or you can just plan on doing better tomorrow.

Because, after all, Leadership Presence is a path, not a destination.

@DrJanice: The real lessons of life happen while you're living it. That's why they're never neat.

Whether or not you have kids, you once were one. And whether or not you remember, you were pretty smart back then. That's the trouble with growing up. In the expansion of your knowledge and experience, there's the risk of forgetting valuable lessons you learned early in life.

Five Leadership Lessons From My Kids

I went to college, and grad school. (More than once, each.) I've attended the training programs and read the books and listened to the podcasts. And despite all of that, when I think about it, I actually learned some of my most important leadership lessons from my kids. So thanks, Andrew and Marni. I'm going to share your primo contributions to my leadership education with the rest of the world.

1. *If people don't want to play with you, it might be more about them than you.*

   Really, I can't count how many times we went through this. Someone chose not to invite my offspring to a play date or club or party, and the world would be coming to an end. But then they grew up. And last week one of them told me where some of those kids are now – more than twenty years later – and you wouldn't want to be there for all the coffee at Starbucks.

   Leadership Lesson: It's more important to be true to yourself than it is to be popular.

2. *Sometimes being silly is more effective than being serious.*

   Oh, how Andrew loved Dr. Seuss! I can still recite parts of *Hop on Pop*, which just shows you how effectively repetition reinforces retention. But buried within the silly was always something really important, meaning it was worth remembering and worth trying to apply in everyday life. As we learned from *Horton*, "A person's a person no matter how small," which was quite useful the day young Andrew met a very small man in a wheelchair. And, with a tip of my pen to the amazing Mr. Geisel… A very important lesson, you see. And to that, I'm sure, we can all agree.

Leadership Lesson: Make your message into a mantra. Make it meaningful, and make it memorable. Then it will stick around long enough to make a difference.

3. *It's important to know the rules other people are trying to follow, even if no one follows them perfectly.*

Life is a little like a square dance. Sometimes you don't know which way to go till someone calls out directions. But, not so for Marni. She was more of a 'Time Warp' girl. (For those unfamiliar with the cult fave movie 'Rocky Horror Picture Show,' Time Warp is a dance…sort of… It has rules, but the excitement of a Rocky Horror gathering often causes members of the youthful crowd to lose track of the difference between 'right' and 'stage right.') Marni knew the steps so well that even in the midst of pandemonium, she could guide and redirect those who got lost.

Leadership Lesson: Leading is only occasionally about where the team is going. Usually it's about where the team is, how it's doing, and helping it to do better.

4. *The best rewards are the ones that make people feel good.*

As the parenting myth goes, treating your kids fairly means treating them equally. This leads to a lot of parenting strategies like what to do when there's only one piece of cake left and the kids are fighting over it. (Neophytes and non-parents, it works like this: one kid divides the cake and the other chooses first.) The trouble with this strategy is that equal quantities may not be what either recipient is really hoping for. Imagine how blessed I felt when I realized that one of my kids preferred the whites of hard-boiled eggs and the other preferred the yolks.

Leadership Lesson: Forget about 'fair' and reward people with what they like best. This will require extra effort – but the results will be more than worth the trouble. Also, when the work has involved vast amounts of collaboration, make sure the rewards are likewise collaborative.

5. *You don't need to fix everything. Sometimes it's best just to tolerate and wait.*

Inevitably, in parenting life, there are times when all the perfection you wish for dissolves into tears. Sometimes it's the kids who have wet faces. Sometimes it's you. It used to happen a lot on those enforced togetherness adventures called 'family vacation.' Two kids and a dog in the back of a station wagon, three days from New York to Florida. Are you getting the picture? When Jean-Paul Sartre wrote, "Hell is other people," you'd swear he was describing road-weary, hungry travelers cooped-up in a tiny motel room with a semi-functioning television set, fighting for the last scrap of the nutritionally questionable swag obtained by a late-night raid on a vending machine. In times like that, sunrise over the ocean and a sandy shore may be all that's needed to restore balance.

Leadership Lesson: Remember that stress happens in times both good and bad. That way, you'll be able to anticipate it, make others ready for it, and keep things under control when it hits.

@DrJanice: If you care, you clue in. You become clueful. And aggregate cluefulness increases.

Name-calling is even more annoying to me than meaningless video games. (I mean the ones whose only purpose is to put other people down or kill them. Or both.) So I don't like it when people say that someone is clueless. Because anyone can become clueful if they just know that it's in the realm of possibility – and they care about it.

Are You Clueful? Do You Care?

I've taken to using the word 'cluefulness' and all its glorious variants because I'm tired of hearing people bandy about phrases like 'he hasn't got a clue' and 'she's the most clueless person I ever had on my staff.' Listen up: that language misses the point, and here's why.

First of all, people who don't have a clue don't realize what they are missing. Duh. (Why would they have a clue about themselves if they don't have a clue about others?)

Second, I realized that it doesn't matter if you have a clue or not. How many times have you found yourself in a situation where you really didn't have a clue? (For me, the first video game after Pong left me in the cold. Blasting Space Invaders and chomping power pills just wasn't an attraction.) *What matters is whether or not you care!*

In the case of video games, I was clueless but I still had to care. Between my two kids, the television was permanently tuned to whichever game one or the other was playing.

I was forced to confront my cluelessness and to try to become clueful.

Guess what. It wasn't that hard. I asked questions. I listened politely. I shook my head, despairing I would ever be clueful enough. And amidst the head shaking, some puzzle pieces must have rattled into place. I realized that my attraction to the game was irrelevant. It was important to my kids, and they were entitled to their own view of the game. And the world. And even their own view of me.

So that solved the problem. Because I cared, I became more clueful, at least where it concerned my job as mom. And, amazingly enough, it also worked at the office.

We can increase cluefulness in our time. We just need to care about it.

@DrJanice: Heaven is having a well-fitting job and well-fitting shoes at the same time. #justsaying

Maybe it's because my mother was always fussing at me with pins and basting thread, but the need for a great fit has been ingrained in me since girlhood. For mom, it was just a nip and a tuck and you were good to go. But when you're trying to fit with a job, it gets a little more complicated than sleeve length and shoulder pads…

Three NEW Questions for Performance Management

A while back, somewhere around the middle of my last book, I posited the idea that there were only three questions any self-respecting executive needed for performance management. To quote myself, these were:

- Are you doing enough of what you like?

- Are you doing too much of what you don't like?

- What can we do to change these things and make them better?

The idea behind this, aside from the fact that *everyone* hates traditional 'bingo card' evaluations, was that if someone isn't doing enough of what they really like then they are probably in the wrong job, looking for another job, not very productive, or all of the above. I also knew that you – the manager providing the performance feedback – could actually help your people do better if you only could work with them and make some small alterations in their scope of responsibility or everyday tasks.

Time has a wonderful way of proving people wrong, if not with a 'sin of commission' at least one of omission. So, *mea culpa*, I will now make up for it. Because, as you'll see, there was one really important thing I forgot to emphasize.

My thinking started to expand one day while on the phone with George Brooks, the leader of EY's People Advisory Services for the Americas. When I asked him what he really wanted, he said, "I just want to be happy at work, and I want the same for my people."

I, of course, immediately fell in love. What could be better than someone who not only wants good for their own life, but for the lives of all they touch every day?

The root of happiness at work, as well as in the rest of life, is in knowing that you have made a positive impact on something, that you have made meaningful contributions. It's nice when they are recognized, but for many, recognition palls next to meaning. In fact, for some, being recognized for something they think is not meaningful is somewhat painful, even when it comes accompanied by a large infusion of cash.

What puts the meaning into our contributions is that they fill a need of something larger than our small selves. That is our one commonality, although, of course, your meaningful contributions will likely be very different than mine. (This is a good thing. I would probably be a hot mess at doing what you do well, so I would not be serving our team in any meaningful, productive way.)

And so, without further ado, the new, improved version of Performance Management:

- Are you doing enough of what your team needs?

- Are you doing too much of what your team does not need?

- What are we going to do to make it better?

Because, as my wise caller knew, when the Team is happy, everyone is happy.

@DrJanice: Hi, I'm Dr. Janice Presser aka DrJ from Philly, architect of #Teamability and tweeting #CEO. And digitally 21. #socialleader

Sometimes I get serious. And nothing is more serious than trying to bring your organization into the Digital Age when leadership is kicking and screaming, holding on to the past. Part of the problem, I think, is that successful digital transformation requires depending on the people you didn't think were as important to the organization as you. Hint: Ask the Team for its thoughts on the subject.

Teaming Dynamics for Digital Transformation

More than half of the companies that were in the Fortune 500 at the turn of this century have either gone bankrupt, been acquired, ceased to exist, or have fallen from the ranks of the 500. All of this disruption was happening as the number of Internet users was tripling, but the challenges (and opportunities) for business were far greater than proliferating websites and e-commerce.

Increasingly, the key factor in a continually accelerating pace of change is the digitalization of business concepts, models, and operating platforms. The process is completely overturning the competitive landscape, even for early winners in the race to web-based business. In some markets, barriers to entry traditionally enjoyed by market leaders have virtually collapsed, and in others it has become more difficult than ever to survive, scale, and eventually dominate a market.

It's clear: business success increasingly demands digital transformation. And digital proficiency is the gateway.

Stages of Digital Proficiency

When you consider the stages of digital proficiency, some interesting parallels with human development begin to emerge.

From birth, socialization starts with our developing sense of the meeting place between self and other, which is really our first foray into teaming. This development happens in four distinct stages, and digital transformation – or at least, our experience of it – is comparable in the way that it unfolds. You might think of digital transformation as representing a new level of consciousness for business, collectively represented by the will of the team to drive the change needed to dominate its industry.

The first stage, **pre-digital awareness**, is analogous to the earliest stage of life, from birth through the first month, when – to the newborn – there is no mommy and no me. When the development of an organization is limited to this state, it is as if there is no awareness of anything outside itself. This leads to no identified cause and effect in customer acquisition, relationships, or retention, as well as little or no use of the digital environment. And, since everything is essentially 'self' at this stage, outreach (teaming with others or collaborating with channels) is not consciously considered.

The second stage is **digital competence**, which maps to human symbiosis. This is the way we view the world until we are about nine months old. In essence, 'mommy and me' are one, in the infant's mind. Consider the way some people react when first introduced to a marvelous new technology. It's as if they are thinking, 'Wow, this technology reads my mind and knows what I want.' Without the ability to rapidly navigate and take control, their experience is analogous to an infant's creeping and crawling. They learn bit by bit, without a coherent overview. This lack of independence supports the feeling that 'we are one,' and thus technology continues to seem magical. In an organization at this stage, even when technology is used, it does not necessarily map to outcomes. True collaboration is not required, only processes, so there is little conscious sense of teaming, either with other people or with the technology.

In the third stage of human relationship development, roughly corresponding to ages 10-18 months, the emphasis is on the

child's **emerging understanding of cause and effect.**
Here the parallels with digital literacy have to do with a
temporary illusion of power that comes from the first taste of
independence. Indeed, it's that same heady feeling you get when
first able to navigate your environment on your own steam,
whether that means getting from the living room to the kitchen,
or generating a list of prospects from your new sales database.
However, in both cases, the connections between action and
outcome have only begun to be made. In organizations, this
phase of development is often stalled by the emergence of silos.
In a highly siloed organization, self-interest may be elevated
above the best interests of the team. Attempts at change can
produce anger, resistance, or even sabotage.

And, just as parents must provide clear and consistent
boundaries as they guide the development of young humans,
clear requirements regarding the current and desired states
of interaction and team dynamics are essential to all Digital
Transformation initiatives. In this fourth stage, which occurs
at the latter end of the second year of human life, there is a
full realization that the individual is, essentially, alone, and
that comfort, connection, and even survival are only possible
through interaction with others. Appropriately, **in human
development this is known as rapprochement**: it ushers
in the growth phase often called 'the terrible twos.' (I prefer
to think of it as the 'terrific twos' because – despite the fallout
that happens due to shortages of parental understanding and/or
patience – it's very important to learn to say no and assert your
independence!)

Organizations in a state of rapprochement have gained
awareness that the digital world is much more complex than
it once seemed to be. In response, the organization begins to
focus on relationships between people who are critical to the
success of change and growth. Today, this includes attention to
the ideal state of digital disruption, and it marks the beginning
of understanding that **complex systems require sustainable,
high-quality teaming**. In fact, we would argue that quality

teaming and a team-friendly environment is a prerequisite for digital disruption.

The fifth and final stage aligns with **social maturity** in humans. It features a constant awareness of self-in-the-team. The organization has developed a transformational business vision that integrates present disruptive technologies, and is prepared to integrate future disruptive technologies as they arise in the marketplace (and/or, as they are developed in-house.) This requires a sustainable, coherent culture and teaming capabilities that are resilient enough to address and process future unexpected and unknowable business disruptions, as well as the resulting opportunities.

The Seven Rules for Digital Business and Digital Transformation

Ray Wang* has given us The Seven Rules For Digital Business and Digital Transformation. Each of Ray's Rules presents a specific challenge to organizational coherence and teaming dynamics. For each one, we see a linkage to organizational needs for more resilient, productive, and meaningful teamwork. These needs are precisely the ones that Teamability® was engineered to fill. The technology not only identifies and organizes person-to-person teaming behaviors, but also the different ways that people seek to serve the team itself, as a living entity. As such, it can provide strong planning, development, and decision support in any transformational situation.

Rule 1: *Digital disruption is more than just a technology shift. It's about transforming business models and how organizations engage.*

First-movers need visionary leaders who can create transformational business models, and who can lead effectively through challenging situations. Teamability can absolutely identify the appropriate teaming behavior and the ability to withstand the ordinary and extraordinary stresses and ambiguities of change.

Rule 2: *We move from selling products and services to keeping brand promises.*

Keeping a brand promise isn't just a directive or a script. A cultural example needs to be built and maintained. There is a certain kind of leader, called a Vision Former, who embodies the conscience, the ethos, of an organization. He or she need not be the CEO, but one or more will be essential on C-level teams. Sadly, that is not always the case – but in the course of Digital Disruption, the absence will be a serious liability.

Rule 3: *We serve five generations of customers and workers, by digital proficiency, not by age.*

The divides between baby boomers, Gen X, Gen Y, Millennials, and others, are certainly relevant in some ways. But the urge to team with others is fundamental to human nature. How well a team interacts with a given technology is related to the way a person seeks to serve team needs (which we call Role, with a capital R) and Coherence (which is the orientation to teaming for a common purpose, no matter the level of stress). How well we share what we know is related to the integrity of the human infrastructure and the Coherence Ratio of the organization.

Digital disruption doesn't happen around the campfire. It happens across time and space. The teams that make it happen need to be able to work that way.

Rule 4: *Data is the foundation of digital business. Every touch point, every click, every digital exhaust is relevant insight.*

The clarity and relevance of the data at the foundations of digital transformation, plus the analytics derived from data systems, will only be as reliable and useful as the development of a human infrastructure allows.

Information drives insight, but the use of insight depends on team awareness (the team being the organization, which includes the elements of teaming required in order to serve its mission, meet customer needs, create brand ambassadors, etc.).

The Vision Movers and Vision Formers in organizations focus on applying information that is big picture and long term, while Action Movers and Action Formers focus on applying tactical information. And, incidentally, as both of these Roles learn to nurture and sustain the presence of a strong Coherence Ratio in their teams (and the entire organization) they will apply that information more effectively and productively.

Rule 5: *If 20% of your revenue is not an insight stream by 2020, you won't have a digital biz model.*

Transforming an insight stream from information source to revenue will require organizations to develop a solid Vision Mover/Vision Former culture that can anticipate and answer the questions of differentiated customer experiences, data brokerage, and other insight-oriented business opportunities.

Rule 6: *You need more than a Chief Digital Officer to infuse digital into your organization. You need a broad bench of Digital CXO's.*

The Chief Digital Officer may be leading the charge, but without a broader bench of Digital CXO's, any digital initiative is in danger of having to fight for resources. It takes more than a General to battle digital stagnation!

At minimum, the C-level team needs to include both Vision Movers and Vision Formers. Vision Movers connect with the vision and drive it forward forcefully, but without a strong Vision Former somewhere on the team, the charge may go in the wrong direction. Someone needs to be the high level arranger/ refiner of disruptive strategies, so that they can be rolled out in elegant and efficient digital initiatives.

But wait, there's more… because planning a fabulous digital strategy doesn't get you there without the help of the right people, the 'digital artisans.'

Rule 7: *We must invest in digital artisans.*

Once the strategic plan is completed, and funded, the digital artisans take over. They not only manage the development cycle and provide the content, but it's also their job to sell everyone on using the value created. This, of course, requires a team, because digital artisans, like their pre-digital forebears, are specialists. And, this is the challenge that organizations will continue to face: the attraction, development, engagement, integration, and retention of these digital artisans. Their value has not previously been fully recognized, but as more organizations vie for them, the market will respond. There will be scarcity, and especially there will be scarcity of the best in their digital crafts.

To a significant degree, digital artisans who are convinced that organizations do not understand or appreciate their value will underperform or leave, exacerbating the shortage. Many of these will have had experiences in larger organizations in which they felt that, like *Dilbert,* they were working for a Pointy Haired Boss. (Note: Understanding someone's Role in the teaming spectrum gives you management insights, especially on how to respect, appreciate, and communicate with them effectively, so they don't experience you as a PHB.)

Key among these digital artisans will be the Explorers, who bring new technologies, methods, and ideas into the organization. Expect a serious shortage of Explorers in your organization – unless you can figure out how to keep them. (Explorers search for treasures and bring them back to benefit their team.) Expressing a sense of wonder and gratitude when they present you with their latest finding is the appropriate way to show thanks and respect to an Explorer. Failing to do so is tantamount to inviting an Explorer to go find a new giftee!

Communicators, those lovable people who feel that their mission is to build communities, online and off, may be easier to retain. However, you will need to identify the right ones – not just for where your organization is now, but also for where you're expecting it to go.

And so on and so forth with the other Roles, because digital artisans are not of a single stripe.

By assembling teams in which the Roles are a particularly good match to the mission of the team, you can automatically improve team coherence. This structural approach is essential when team members are virtual.

Balanced teams with a coherence level appropriate to the amount of stress and challenge, and contextually useful Teaming Characteristics, will recognize and support each team member while integrating their value into the whole. The results: positive engagement, productive collaboration, resilience, quality, and exceptional productivity.

The Many Roles of Digital / Social Technologies

As an aside, good digital/social technology can fill or support a specific Role – just like people do – on a team. Truly great digital/social technology can fill and support more than one Role. Here are some examples, and the Role-support they provide:

- **Waze**, as Explorer and Curator, and it can also function as Communicator

- **Evernote**, in support of everyone, but especially the Vision Roles, acts as Action Former and/or Curator, depending on how you primarily use it

- **Twitter** can function as your Conductor via its instant give and take, which connects you to crowdsourced quick fixes

- **LoseIt** is a Watchdog that minds best interest of your health, as do similar Internet of Things technologies

- **Just about any to-do list app** is the Action Mover's best friend, almost as good as a real live Action Former

- Any community-boosting app, such as **Facebook** or **LinkedIn** ultimately functions as a Communicator.

Using Teamability to Build a Culture of Digital Artisans

Prior to the emergence of Teamability, you could measure what occurs inside people – what they think they're thinking, what they think they value, what they think they're like, and how they think they will behave. But, you often needed a licensed psychologist to sign off on it.

Teamability is disruptive technology in the form of a deceptively simple serious game. It doesn't ask you what you think you know or what you think you feel or value. It puts you in a situation – a simulation of teaming – and as you interact with other characters in the scenario, the boundaries between your world and the digital world begin to dissolve. This makes it possible to directly access and measure teaming behavior.

The ultimate outcome will be a coherent human infrastructure, achieved through the Teamability experience and proprietary team analysis and management methods. It will guide the selection, development, and nurturance of all, including digital artisans, engaging them in work that aligns with their deepest desire to make a meaningful team contribution, and virtually 'gluing' them in place.

* R 'Ray' Wang is the Principal Analyst & Founder of Constellation Research, and author of Disrupting Digital Business: Create an Authentic Experience in the Peer-to-Peer Economy, HBR Press, 2015.

@DrJanice: If you have to smuggle #innovation past your manager, they don't want it. Oh dear.

I was inspired to write this on my way home after a speaking gig at Sapphire/ASUG, the annual conference held by software giant SAP. Just me and 19,999 other people who might talk about innovation, but who mostly just do it. And that's where cool new stuff comes from. Yes, I was with people who do more doing than talking, and that was a breath of fresh air.

Can We Please Stop Talking About Innovation and Just Do It?

I'm not opposed to dreaming up cool new stuff, understand. I do a good bit of it myself, which is how Teamability® got born. But I never talked about innovation as if it were the answer to some cosmic problem.

Get this straight, leaders. People create. Even you, the one who first mixed peanut butter and jelly on bread because that was all you had on the shelf. You may not think of yourself as a creator, but you are.

Note that I am <u>not</u> using the adjective form 'creative.' Let me tell you why.

An adjective is used to describe and qualify, and that makes it hard to argue with someone who thinks this or that description doesn't really fit. You have to start by defining your terms and by the time you're done hacking your way through verbal kudzu, you're too tired to make anything happen. But when you use verbs, you bypass all that.

Forget being creative. Forget being innovative. And please forget trying to teach people to be either. Just stop interrupting them when they're creating. Or innovating. Or even disruptively innovating. And stop putting roadblocks in their way.

If crowdsourcing has taught us one thing, it's that a team is able to create much more, much faster, than any one person can. Ever. No matter how smart they are. Even if they are, or think they are, creative. Or innovative. Or disruptive.

If you want to innovate, just ask the right people on your team to get the process going. But don't make them responsible for getting much else actually done.

Fans of Teamability know that it's simple: match job responsibility to Role. (For the uninitiated, 'Role' is a person's innate mode of serving organizational needs.)

To go for something completely different, ask your Founders. (They aren't necessarily the people who started the company, but it's likely that at least one of them will be.) In Teamability terms, Founders are people who dream up new stuff; grand visions. Sometimes it's successful and sometimes it isn't. But that's how Founders serve the Team.

If you are looking for a key piece of something that you think might exist, or does exist but you don't know where, go ask your Explorers. In Teamability terms, these are people who deeply feel that 'serving the team' means going off into the field (be it real-world or cyberspace) and finding things that will benefit others. Sometimes they bring back treasures that are exactly what you needed, and sometimes you just won't know what to do with them. (The treasures, I mean, not the Explorers. I'll get to what to do with Explorers in a moment.)

Then take what you've got – a big idea or a fabulous find – hand it over to the team, and get out of their way.

Meanwhile, it's your job to make sure your Founders and Explorers are appreciated, rewarded, and respected for the way they contribute. And that's much easier than you might think.

Your Founders need to feel your support for their big vision. They probably care less about extra dollars in their paycheck than they do about having the project solidly funded. Without grumbling. If you give the right kind of respect, they will respond with more passion, more loyalty, more hard work, and even bigger, better ideas the next time you ask.

Your Explorers need something that's not any harder to provide than what works for Founders. It's just different. When they bring you a treasure, you need to show them (say it!) that you are impressed or even astounded by their ability to locate such a wondrous thing. Acknowledge that they have been diligent in bringing it back to you. Remember, if it doesn't match your heart's desire, you don't have to use it. Just appreciate it. That's how to respect an Explorer. And if it does work out and brings profits to the organization, would you please remember them and repeat the message? This will ensure that they don't forget you when they're on their next expedition.

Now you've got your work cut out for you. Stop talking and start doing!

@DrJanice: If you think 'meh' too many times a day, you might not be living your optimal life. #justsaying

People like to take tests that feed back to them what they just said. I don't know why. (I ask questions. However, unlike lawyers, I don't always have the answers before I ask.) Sometimes it's just a better way to get ideas across, so if you hate taking tests, just read the questions and don't bother answering them. Because really, you already know.

Do You Work in a Culture of Mehdiocrity?

No, my spell checker is not out of order. In fact, I had to fight to get it to stop correcting me.

Mehdiocrity: *A state of being wherein the only acceptable alternatives are to be non-reactive, to be unengaged, or to raise indifference to an art form.*

There's a lot of it going around.

Mehdiocrity is not as simple as mediocrity.

With mediocrity, you get a result. And if your team is truly mediocre, it's probably a result that's repeatable and reliable. This condition is even built in to the quality standards of ISO 9000: the product doesn't have to be excellent, just consistent. Work gets done in a mediocre culture, but it doesn't make your heart sing.

Mehdiocrity is much different.

It has nothing to do with intelligence, talents, abilities, skills, values, ethics, emotions, or personality. In fact, it's totally cultural. By which I mean contextual, and not related to where you grew up or how your family celebrates birthdays. It's not you: it's your work environment. Perhaps the cause is stagnant growth, lack of healthy competition, or stultifying business processes. But it's often said that 'people don't leave companies, they leave managers'…so it could be your boss.

Right now, you're probably wondering, so here's how to find out.

The Mehdiocrity Test:

Just answer yes or no. No maybes. (That would be mediocre.)

1. I don't know what the purpose of my job is and I have given up trying to figure it out.

2. I only receive praise for things I don't care about and for accomplishments that I can't actually remember ever doing.

3. My opinions only count when they match those of my manager and the people around me who my manager is favoring at the moment.

4. I use my allowed leave time as soon as it is granted, since I feel I must have regular 'mental health' days.

5. While I may occasionally have opportunities for learning, I don't bring the knowledge back to my business unit because it might conflict with the unyielding mindset of my manager.

6. When my colleagues at work ask me 'How's it going?' the only honest answer I could give (but usually don't) is "meh…"

Scoring: Yes = 0 or 1, are you hiring? Yes = 2, merely mediocre; Yes = 3 or 4, uh-oh; Yes = 5 or 6, go to YouTube immediately for Lewis Black rant-therapy.

OK. Now you know. What are you going to do about it?

Remember it's just your environment. You could leave. Or you could plan to leave. Or maybe you are still thinking that the money and benefits are worth it.

These days, not many people have the luxury of a quick exit. Where you work, the people who were able to leave at will have already left. So let's assume you're going to stay. Here are three steps to preserving what's left of your life force while you figure things out.

- First, make sure to be doing something outside of work that is not mehdiocre.

- Second, find things you can do (without being noticed) at work that are important and beneficial. Think 'stealth productivity.'

- Third, make sure you are fighting on the side of the angels by doing things that leave the world just a little bit better. And when you do, don't forget to reward yourself!

Got any mental health days left?

@DrJanice: Chemical reactions are predictable. So is Team Chemistry. #Teamability

You can't use a barometer to measure temperature. It requires a thermometer. That doesn't make one instrument more or less valuable than the other – except when you want to answer a specific question. When it comes to Team Chemistry, think valence. (Or, as Italian scientist Amedeo Avogadro probably never said, 'Hey Ladies, take my number.')

You Want Team Chemistry? Start with Biology and Physics!

Forbes' publisher Rich Karlgaard drew a line in the sand when he launched an article entitled *Teams Matter, Talent Is Not Enough*. And then along came the brilliant research of Adam Grant, set forth in his NY Times best-seller *Give and Take*. Dr. Grant proved that, contrary to a particularly nasty old adage, nice people frequently finish <u>first</u>.

I see these two writings (and waves of commentary along the same lines) as the beginning of the end of the 'hire-only-the-best-and-brightest' era. For the longest time, hiring has been all about talents, traits, skills, education, and experience. Now, we're returning to a more complex and enlightened place in which the way a person teams is gaining attention and awareness for its critical value.

People speak wistfully about 'team spirit' as if it were a kind of magic spell that could be cast by only the most enlightened of leaders or coaches. Now the phrase 'team chemistry' is coming back into vogue, and that's a lot closer to the truth. Teamwork does indeed embody chemistry.

Not 'I like you' chemistry. Real hard-science chemistry, and biology, and physics.

Biology has given you some inborn drives. One of them drives you to learn and master your world. Another drives you to connect with other people. Put the two together and you get the basic reason humans form teams. Including, by the way, that most basic of teams: the twosome.

Physics, which is essentially the science of how stuff works, explains a lot about the way to build a physical structure (or infrastructure) that won't collapse when an earthquake or tornado hits. Think of what that takes. Strong parts connect with other strong parts in a very strong way. (Okay, that won't get you an engineering degree, but it's at the core of building anything complex. And you can't have a team with just one person, right? You've got the drift?)

For the moment, let's just focus in on that 'very strong connect' part. In human beings, that's called interdependency. It's what causes us to lean on each other and not topple over when bad things happen – like economic tremors causing our employer's 'Richter scale' to register above 4.5.

So, just to review before we get to the midterms…

We have people with fundamental biological drives, which vary. (We can measure that variance, thanks to a new team science that applies to any team in any kind of organization.) And these drives operate within the framework of a team, and fundamental elements of teamwork, which follow the rules of physics.

Now we're ready to tackle chemistry.

Even if high school or college chemistry is just a faded memory for you, you might be familiar with the principle of valence, aka covalent bonding. Or (depending on when you went to school) molecular orbital theory, which begat modern valence bond theory. No matter the name, or the level of detail in scientifically explaining how atoms form molecules, valence is about attraction. The most important thing you need to know about attraction between two entities is that it happens because there are physical forces that come into play to balance out an unstable imbalance. This creates 'completeness.'

When you understand the teaming energy that is inherent in each person on the team, then you can predict the focus and drive they will apply to the fulfillment of specific team needs (Role). You can also predict the way they will handle adversity, change, or just plain old stress, in service to the team's mission (Coherence).

Ready for team chemistry? Here's the formula:

In humans, 'completeness' happens on a team after you get the right biology — people motivated to do something big with a team — into the right physical configuration.

Since each Role exhibits a complementary (balancing and energizing) influence on one other Role, add only the Roles that are most appropriate to the team's mission, and introduce them all to each other so that each can find their natural 'Role-pair' by virtue of complementary forces of attraction.

Then step back and watch the sparks fly!

@DrJanice: Coherence won't cohere you, but it might make it easier for you to stick around.

When you come from a place of valuing science and scientific method, you tend to rely on it to explain everything that's not quite right in the world. So, because my favorite step in research is crafting the operational definitions, I tend to get a little touchy when people violate their boundaries. Then I remember, these are operational definitions. And I remember, those are never really self-explanatory.

Cohesion, Coherence, Clarity, and Connectedness

I've always been a bit of a stickler for language. Not quite so much as Humpty Dumpty, who says to Alice during her adventures in Wonderland (a place with disturbing similarities to the 9 to 5 worlds that some of us inhabit): "When I use a word... it means just what I choose it to mean – neither more nor less." For me, words are nuanced, and specific – not used as a device of control but for the purpose of communicating new ideas by connecting them to things that people already understand.

Having said that, please know that I'm not upset when people use 'cohesion' when they are talking about 'coherence.' It's only in the interest of clarity that I'm even mentioning it.

Cohesion is the state of sticking together. On a team, cohesion accurately describes the traditional sense of everyone doing the same thing at the same time. (No I will not say "hold hands and sing Kumbaya," but if you thought of that, you've got the idea.) That kind of cohesion worked best back when there was one boss and he (it was almost always 'he') made all the decisions, and large numbers of people were actually doing the same thing.

On many modern teams, teammates are far less likely (than they were, say, 20 years ago) to be doing the same thing; and even less likely to be working in the same building, or state, or country. In the future of work, cohesion - marching in lockstep - will be of less and less value. Team members will need to be able to handle the stress that comes with collaborating through distance, ambiguity, and continuous change. What they will need is coherence.

Coherence is physical. It's a term used in signal processing, which involves a lot of equations. (Once upon a time, I wanted to become a theoretical mathematician. I like the elegance of equations, but I fear that the vast majority of you may not, so there won't be any here.) Think of what it's like when you have a bad phone connection, causing noise and distortion of the sound. That signal has low coherence, so it's easy to recognize that coherent sound is highly desirable.

Lasers emerged when scientists learned how to generate a coherent beam of light, and lasers are now used in electronics, entertainment, medicine, and communications. The laser that's used for surgery allows the surgeon to pinpoint, with extreme precision, the place that gets cut. If you ever need eye surgery, you'll appreciate this, because it makes for relatively pain-free recovery.

But did you know that a beam of laser light, projected from Earth to the Moon – a quarter of a million miles away – will light up an area that is just a mile and a quarter in diameter? Compare that with a normal flashlight beam, which begins to spread out mere inches from the source. Even the beam from a powerful searchlight can be seen to fade away.

When I use the term coherence to describe how people team, I'm talking about the same phenomenon. When people operate coherently, they have 'clean' relationships with the others on their team. If needed, they can all take on different jobs within the team, moving to more leadership if that's their specialty, and hanging back to let others step up when it's the right time. The clarity and intensity that accompany the state of Coherence is what keeps people attracted to, and feeling a part of, their team – no matter where in the world they may be.

Now what does all this have to do with connectedness?

It turns out that a lot of our daily work, and a lot of the 'content' that happens in the course of organizational activity, is subject to the influence of nodes in a social network. In particular, those would be the high-level nodes known as 'hubs,' which represent the people who seem to know everyone, and through whom a lot of communication passes.

When social nodes are Coherent, they are free of noise and distortion. The signal that enters them is pretty much the same as the one that emerges. But a message can change when it passes through a less coherent node. The result could be a simple misunderstanding, a significant error, or a layer of political intrigue. Either way, the network maintains connectedness, but a coherent network is one that is better tuned to nurturing people, amplifying performance, and maintaining the integrity of the organization and its vision.

So let's strive for the clarity and connectedness that comes with coherence. Beyond that, cohesion is optional.

@DrJanice: I give to my friend and I get something back. I give to my Team and the world gets something back.

I'm not opposed to giving, I just hate 'keeping score' so I don't do it. But I am pretty sure I'm in the minority there, given the number of people who use apps to track things like this and who 'unfriend' you if you don't follow their every move. This piece was inspired after a conversation with the charming Dr. Grant about how to multiply the positive effects of giving with an open heart.

Giving and Taking and More

We all like to think of ourselves as 'givers' but as Dr. Adam Grant, author of NY Times and Wall Street Journal bestseller, *Give and Take* (and more recently *Originals*) has said, "Generosity is earned, not claimed."

For the most part – and to most people – giving is just giving. However, there is a big difference between giving to one other person and giving to your team.

Dr. Grant's research has given us a broadly applicable understanding of what goes on in person-to-person giving. Having identified the key players as Givers, Takers, and Matchers, the effect (often surprising) that each type of participant has on the other two becomes clear. He has also described the impact that these three modes of interaction can have on organizational culture in general, and I for one am all-in! Who wouldn't prefer a culture of giving to one of taking?

Giving to (or taking from) another person has a concrete sensibility. It also calls for a human act of courtesy and/or closure, in the form of reciprocation. Givers give without any expectation of thanks or repayment, but culturally we have learned to give back, and few would fail to take note of an earnest 'thank you.' Matchers, being attuned to the balance between giving and taking, are very likely to notice whether or not reciprocation has occurred. And hard-core Takers, who may have no intention of giving anything meaningful in return, will take care to verbally reciprocate in order to maintain their guise as a Giver or Matcher.

But when it comes to 'Team giving,' the plot thickens.

When people give-and-take with each other, the exchange is person-to-person. But in a very real and significant way, 'the Team' is like a living entity with needs of its own, and can also give and take. The nature of this exchange is person-to-team, but the team (being a conceptual construct) cannot say 'Thank you.' Instead, your 'reward' is the satisfaction of an inner need to make a team contribution.

Most people have a specific sense of what 'making a meaningful contribution' is. It varies from person to person, but generally aligns with a specific team need. We call this distinct sense of purpose a person's 'Role' – with a capital R – and the greatest reward for 'team giving' comes when the nature of the giving is aligned with the giver's Role. When other Roles are also giving to (serving) the team in this way, the communal sense of wellbeing becomes very strong. Why? Because giving one-to-one is a simple exchange. When you give to the team, you answer a higher calling. This is the essence of 'team spirit.'

So, in comparing the dynamics of person-to-person giving to those of 'team giving,' our attention shifts from 'how much and how often' to 'where,' 'why,' and 'to what end.'

With that understanding, here are the ways the ten different Roles give to their team:

Founders give Inspiration. Inspiration is distinct from Positive Programming (see Vision Formers, below) in that Founders seek to attract a desired mode of teaming, not to directly access and shape it.

Vision Movers give Direction. While some people (Vision Movers, in particular) don't like the idea of being directed, it is a welcome gift to people with other Roles, who can then contribute with the assurance that their group is on a proper course to the goal. Direction is 'advice on steroids.'

Vision Formers give Positive Programming, defined as fostering desired attitudes about people and teams, and their future productive behaviors.

Action Movers give Service, which is why they make excellent first responders and other kinds of 'get it done' people. Some people think of doing service as the equivalent of selflessness, but for an Action Mover, service and self are completely intertwined.

Action Formers give Discipline, which in the world of work, you can think of as organizing, structuring, and setting limits.

Explorers give Unexpected Treasures. These are things that you didn't even know you needed – but which often turn out to be 'just the thing.' What an Explorer brings might be as simple as a hilarious new joke, as exciting as the first look at a tremendous business opportunity, or as vital as early warning of danger ahead.

Watchdogs give Nurturance, which consists of accepting, validating, and caretaking behaviors. They often give mentoring right along with anything else they're doing for the team.

Conductors give Solutions. They focus on short-term problem solving and making things work better. The word 'hack' – the application of ingenuity to a puzzle or problem – is a fit to what the Conductor likes to do. However, Conductors are wedded to expediency. If it works, it's good. Longer-term consequences are of comparatively little concern to the Conductor.

Curators give Wisdom, which often serves as the link to deeper thinking, to more creative problem solving, to guidance from past experience, and to the avoidance of pitfalls.

Finally, **Communicators give Information**. Let's be clear that in giving to a team, information is to the Communicator as wisdom is to the Curator. At times the information might sound like gossip, but that's not what Communicators do. Their activity comes from the desire to connect (or reconnect) people with *the vision and mission of the team*, and also with each other to create a common bond. Quite literally, Communicators build communities.

These ideas on giving are offered freely as a creative spark for further inquiry into giving, taking, and teaming. A better understanding of collaborative team structures will make it possible to design teams and organizational cultures in which greater giving and meaningful work are available to all. And that, after all, is the goal of The Gabriel Institute, and the life purpose of its founders.

@DrJanice: You learn the past to live in the present and plan for the future. Focus on one at a time.

Part 3: Everything

By now it's probably clear that I have a big vision; a very positive one. I believe that the world really can be moved toward universal peace and understanding, and that Teamability® is one of the levers that will help it happen.

"Too many of us leave our lives — and, in fact, our souls — behind when we go to work."
> — *Arianna Huffington*

"The most meaningful way to succeed is to help others succeed."
> — *Adam Grant*

"If you think you are too small to make a difference, try sleeping with a mosquito in the room."
> — *Dalai Lama*

"The most we can hope for is to create the best possible conditions for success, then let go of the outcome. The ride is a lot more fun that way."
> — *Phil Jackson*

"Motivation comes from working on things we care about. It also comes from working with people we care about."
> — *Sheryl Sandberg*

"Lesson: In the real world, ninety-nine cents will not get you into New York City. You will need the full dollar."
— *Bruce Springsteen*

"Life is not a solo act. It's a huge collaboration, and we all need to assemble around us the people who care about us and support us in times of strife."
— *Tim Gunn*

"We must all hang together, or assuredly, we shall all hang separately."
— *Ben Franklin*
(at the signing of the Declaration of Independence)

"I dream of a better tomorrow, when chickens can cross the road and not be questioned about their motives."
— *Anonymous*

"The shortest distance between two people…is laughter.
— *Victor Borge*

"I tell the kids, Someone's gotta win. Someone's gotta lose. Don't fight about it. Just try to get better."
— *Yogi Berra*

"Individually, we are one drop. Together, we are an ocean."
— *Ryunosuke Satoro*

@DrJanice: Never ask a question you don't already know the answer to. Just know if you are not a lawyer, life will be boring.

Studies say we now spend even more of our lifetime hours at work. And most of us work in environments that sap our strength, our power, our hope — and in the worst ones, our very reason for being. And it is all so unnecessary. In fact, I look forward to the day when I never again ask this question because I already know the answer is a resounding NO!

Is Your Workplace a 'Suckritocracy'?

I had better set a good example here. I take no credit for the word 'suckritocracy' but seriously, doesn't it describe at least one place you've worked?

I heard it attributed to Edith Waltz, a design professor and sociologist who morphed into a business process analyst for Fortune 500 companies. In her experience, those companies were not meritocracies. They were not even aristocracies, and they certainly weren't democracies. They were, pure and simple, suckritocracies – where the people who suck are the ones who get ahead. And, apparently, in her experience, few people cared.

Call me Pollyanna, but I really meant it when I wrote The Gabriel Institute's vision line – Making the Workplace a Better Place to Work.

So in that spirit, I ask you to join me in a revolution to banish this scourge of working life. Here are the three 'rules of engagement':

- First, believe that we can end suckritocracy in our lifetime. All we have to do is to stop contributing to it. Don't take credit for other people's work and, if you can, share the credit that other people give you – whether you think they deserve it or not. Being known as a team player is worth more to your career than being known for being smart.

- Second, figure out what you really like to do and try to work with other people who will do the parts you don't like. If you get yelled at for that, it means the suckritocracy you are working in has hardened into something like the corporate equivalent of 'Zombies from Outer Space.' It eats fear and it can only survive by creating that fear in its young. Your best defense is to starve it.

- Finally, rock your own world. Find the rest of your team. They are out there. (This is something like finding true love.) Respect them. Trust them. Build something wonderful together. (Think Steve & Woz. Hewlett & Packard. Ben & Jerry.)

People who are great at sucking up attention, credit, praise, and power, leaving the real work to others, can't be beaten at their own game. But they can be overwhelmed!

@DrJanice: I love independence but I love interdependence even more. #happy4th

I always loved the ending of the Declaration of Independence, and not just on the Fourth of July. Values that are worth declaring that we "mutually pledge to each other our Lives, our Fortunes and our sacred Honor" are those that are in service to something greater than ourselves. In this case, it was the separation and coming into being of an independent entity, The United States of America. From its beginning as political startup, one might say, the USA has gone on to survive internal discord, external attack, and a major values debate at least every four years. While the desire for independence is what brought the fifty-six signers together, I wonder if perhaps an even deeper desire for interdependence was embedded in the document that remains – to this day – a guidepost and an inspiration to all.

In Our Team We Trust

No, you did not read that wrong. And yes, we'll still be celebrating the Fourth of July, aka Independence Day, in remembrance of our country's successful break with Mother England.

As a culture, we've always been pro-independence. Think of our heroes. The Lone Ranger. Indiana Jones. Mad Men's Don Draper. Even the Shark Tank investors. All act decisively, and they consult no one before acting.

We care so much about independence that we've come to vilify the opposite. Being dependent is synonymous with not being an adult, and being co-dependent is considered pathetic.

Independence makes it lonely at the top…and also in the middle. But there is an alternative: the path of interdependence.

Consider these ideas, all very personal to me, but also, I believe, universal:

- We need to acknowledge our interdependence, to connect with each other, as if our very lives depend on it. Because they do.

- The world needs a new mission that is based not on the ideologies and geographies and histories that divide us, but rather, on our shared, fundamental drive to bond together for the satisfaction of human needs, for the progress of our enterprises, and, perhaps, for our very survival. The new mission will call for meaningful, sustainable, freely chosen giving. And for the mission to succeed, teamwork will become essential. Not just the word 'teamwork,' but a new dynamic of being, governed by meaningful, sustainable, mutual understanding of team contribution.

- People need to be respected for the manner in which they make meaningful contributions to the team. Different people make different kinds of contributions, and some are more visible and seemingly more important than others. But all contributions must be valued highly, because it is a fact that in the life of a team, all contributions are equally valuable.

Teaming and Love are not far apart. They were meant for each other.

@DrJanice: Being too afraid to make sure you have the right team is the road to failure at any level. #leadership

The numbers experts back me up: over half of management hires — internal and external — are not successful, according to the companies that hired them. Need I say more? That means we are, collectively, closer to 100% failing than we are to 0%.

Three Ways to Fail at Management

I grew up in a home where both mom and dad were active union members, and it gave me a clear message about working life: there is labor, and there is management. Labor's job is to make stuff happen. Management's job is to oppress labor.

I was fine with that worldview for a long time. But eventually, I grew up and, somewhere along the line, I *became* management. I even got to <u>like</u> being management. The funny thing is that my parents, the union loyalists, are the ones I have to thank for that. Here's why: they didn't just teach me that oppression was a bad thing. They also made me realize that it can be just as bad for the oppressor as it is for the oppressed.

Oppression is the hallmark of bad management. It's the butt of Dilbertesque jokes about pointy haired bosses and evil functionaries, and it's the bane of workers at all levels of organizations. Typically, oppressors are actively engaged in doing what they do, so it's easy to vilify them for committing crimes against the workplace.

Sins of commission by management are many. Sins of omission are few, but they can be every bit as demoralizing. Here are three that I will address *ad seriatum*. (That's Latin for, *'I'm going to do this one at a time, because hitting you with all three, and no breaks in between, would be seriously uncool.'*)

First, there is failure to observe. You might remember something like this happening early in your working life. It happened to Stacy on her very first job.

The team had a serious problem. Stacy was new, and bright, and identified a solution. It was simple, and it would have worked, but the manager couldn't see it. Boss only saw Stacy, barely 21 years old, too new to know the score, and without a resume to provide credibility. Being laughed at and chided for offering such a naïve opinion was deeply humiliating, and to this day Stacy is reluctant to make suggestions.

Second: failure to nurture. Ari works as an analyst in the innovation department of a huge maker of scientific products. Ari applied three times for the company's 'high potential' program, but the manager never followed through, and Ari was passed over each time. Ari is creative, smart, and well liked. The manager is not. Did the manager feel threatened, or was it just laziness? No matter. Ari has given up.

And third: failure to acknowledge. And herein lies a particularly sad story. Morgan has been in a supervisory position in a critical functional area of an organization for over two years. If you ask the team members, you'll get nothing but glowing reports. But the manager gives no recognition, or support, or praise of any kind. Morgan feels unliked, weak, and fearful of job loss. Despite having opportunities to leave, and to move up, Morgan stays. Why? Because Morgan is there to serve the team and does not give up easily. And also because, in leaving, the team would no longer have a shield from the icy chill of the boss' indifference.

Many failures are just learning experiences, but the failure of management to team well – as exemplified here – causes real damage.

So, if your work experience resonates strongly with that of Stacy, or Ari, or Morgan… *or their managers!* – then beware. When leaders fail to team, they eventually lead a business to fail.

@DrJanice: Sometimes it seems like the Internet is full of reruns. Maybe it's a new show called Breaking Copyright.

I'm not pining for the 'good old days' because really, they weren't any better than now. And, of course, my hope springs eternal for the future. But can we just remember that building that future is going to require connections between people, and that takes more than technology, no matter how smart it is?

In the Internet of Things, Please Don't Forget the People!

When I was a very young mother (and this was a very, very long time ago) my mantra was 'people are more important than things.' It worked the way a good mantra should, as an all-purpose stress reducer. It was especially handy after some bauble had been broken by the crashing of a particular toddler into a coffee table, or to calm things down after that same toddler started pounding on a sibling with a purloined toy. In other words, my mantra served equally as a reminder to myself, and as an influence on the moral development of my offspring.

People before things. I think it's still worthy of consideration.

The other day, a former pro football player-turned-consultant told me about what goes on in the locker room when the team is not on the field. I have to admit, I was doubly disappointed. There were no lurid tales of cheerleaders gone wild; nor were there any heart-warmers about player's moms showing up with homemade chicken soup or huckleberry pie. Not even a kid with cancer getting an autographed shirt from her sports idol. Nope. It was mostly the same as what goes on in the average living room these days: just individuals communing with their tablets and smartphones. Oh, dear.

'But wait,' you say, 'they can't all just be playing games! There's Facebook and Twitter, sending selfies on Instagram, and texting, too.' Yes, these pastimes do give the impression of social activity, but even then they may not actually be social, because no matter how many friends or followers you've amassed, you're alone with yourself and mostly sending one-way signals. There is no guarantee, and rarely an immediate way to know, whether or not even one person has seen, thought about, or cared what you just did.

Compare that with having a face-to-face conversation.

I can understand the appeal, having come of age during the time of beatnik culture. (This was before hippies, and way, way before the dawn of hip-hop.) Back then, alienation had been raised to an art form, but poetry was recited in coffee houses and listeners snapped their fingers to signify that the message was received, processed, and appreciated. There were creators, critics, patrons, and fans, in person and active on the typical team.

Today, we have an Internet that can (and does) bring people together from all around the world to support a cause or to crowdfund a startup business, and websites that personalize the user experiences of even casual visitors. But are these really personal connections – or just sophisticated transactions? The buzz-phrase 'Internet of Things' refers to an Internet populated by inanimate objects that can be tracked and managed remotely. I don't think it was meant to include people, but I worry if that might be where it's headed.

As the word Alchemy describes the work of transforming base metals to gold, Dr. Joshua Lederberg coined the term 'Algeny' to describe the upgrading of human organisms to generate better performance. In terms of giving people more knowledge, more range, and greater potential, the Internet of Things may seem to be a sort of 'Algenist's Apprentice.' But like the Sorcerer, whose errant Apprentice misused powers that he didn't fully comprehend, perhaps we should be aware. Not hostile or fearful.

Just aware.

Consider this: the aforementioned football players are surrounded by people whose job it is to polish and reinforce the interconnectedness of self, others, and team success. Their solitary communion with the Internet of Things is regularly augmented by green grass and a chalk-lined gridiron where (in an immediate and physical way) they crash headlong into their Reality of Teaming.

Yes, I have just capitalized Reality and Teaming. For those of us who are 'on our own' in exploring and experiencing the disembodied existence made possible within the Internet and all of its things, Reality and Teaming may well turn out to be the saving graces.

@DrJanice: There is no glass ceiling if you start at the top. One more reason for a woman to start a company. #justsaying

Back in the early seventies, my daughter was born, just three years after her brother. I promised them both that I would always love them for who they were, that neither would ever be more important to me, nor would I ever favor one over the other. But the reality is, no matter how many bras may have been burned in the 1970's, the promise of equality has never filtered into the culture at large. Even now, more than 40 years later…

Reflections on – and in – Glass Ceilings

I read that line this morning in an article praising the glory of entrepreneurship and I thought, that really describes my life now. I mean, no one ever would have promoted me to CEO. I wouldn't even have been considered a good 'diversity candidate.' (A diversity candidate, I've been told, is one who makes it slightly easier to tell the rest of the finalists apart.) And in addition to that pesky second X chromosome that I carry around, the typical CEO is in the neighborhood of a foot taller than me.

All things considered, it was just easier to start a company and give myself the title, although I have to admit that at the time, no one else wanted it.

On a more serious note, even self-made women CEOs experience well-documented challenges. Try googling "women founders getting venture capital," and you'll see what I mean. It's just a fact that many of the places where you're expected to 'pay your dues' have a sign hanging on the door that says 'No girls allowed.' (Not literally, of course, but savvy women have no trouble reading between the lines.)

After mulling these things over for a while, the whole line of thinking began to bother me. Like I normally do when I need a reality check, or just someone to bounce my ideas off of, I went to Mark, my Vision Former.

Let me take a moment aside to explain that term. My company created Teamability®, a completely new technology that analyzes and organizes teams based on each person's innate affinity for serving a specific organizational need. In the language of Teamability, the name of each capital-R 'Role' in a team suggests the organizational influence the person will most effectively exert. For example, if you have a grand vision, and have even started a company and gotten it off the ground, you are probably a Founder or a Vision Mover…or perhaps both. If so, you haven't lived till you've worked with a top-flight Vision Former, who is your perfect complement and counterbalance.

Now back to the story. I said to Mark, "Maybe I just have never paid my dues like people think they have to, and maybe it's the dues-paying which is why women are frustrated in typical organizations." And he disagreed.

One good thing about having someone whose Role complements yours is that you not only expect the occasional disagreement, you welcome it. It means that by the time you work it out (which you always do) you will both truly and lastingly agree on what makes the most sense.

I should mention that Mark's been a serial entrepreneur since he started (at age 20), built, and sold his first successful business. "Really," he said, "there's been plenty of dues-paying for both of us." He went on to say that the 'no glass ceiling' phrase – while catchy – isn't entirely true, and that there's a glass ceiling for everyone who isn't a winner in the 'lucky sperm club,' i.e., born into money and/or power. (And of course we know that the dues in that club are sometimes extracted in other, even less desirable, ways.)

The Vision Former continued: "There's no quick or easy fix for women (or men) who are frustrated and want to move up in typical organizations. Entrepreneurship can be an escape route, but (using our own startup experience an example) look at how crazy you have be in order to take it! Also, the fascination with entrepreneurship plays into the fantasy that life is better and all will be wonderful at the top. It inherently supports an economically hierarchical model of happiness that really doesn't work for everyone."

Role-fit (aligning a person's 'Role' to their job responsibilities) is the first step to happiness on the job, because it makes a sense of meaningful contribution intrinsic to one's activity. After that, happiness is increased when an organization (including one that you own) understands and facilitates Team-fit and Role-pairings (like the aforementioned Vision Mover/Vision Former). Further down the road, building a team (or a town, or a society) where each person understands and practices Role-respect will open the door to group happiness. All along the way, Coherence gains in strength and influence, and Teaming comes into full bloom.

In full Founder mode, I countered Mark with "I didn't pay dues, I made an investment." Hah! Sounded good to me.

But Mark convinced me that while that was true, and although we had both made big investments in what we believed in, there had still been plenty of dues to pay along the way. (Did I mention that Vision Formers cleave unto Truth and Virtue?) And then he had the temerity to list them for me! We had the craziness! We saw visions! We had the latitude and the tolerance for risking a breakout, so we did! We also had, between the two of us, a ton of just the right kinds of experience, and a genius product!

According to StatisticBrain.com, 44% of new businesses fail within 3 years, and in 76% of the cases, the top reason is incompetence (45%), followed by unbalanced experience and lack of management expertise (30%).

"It's the people," said the VF, "not the business."

So the widespread practice of encouraging people to be entrepreneurial even though they may not have the 'equipment' for the task (or any way to find out whether or not they have it, or where to get it) is not so different from a football coach moving a quarterback to the D-line. It makes no sense, and the outcome is liable to be ugly.

Of course, there can be a big advantage in starting and/or being in an entrepreneurial company. It is the opportunity (maybe) to discover who you are and what you really like to do, and that comes from having to serve the organization as Chief cook-and-bottle-washer (or VP or Director of cooking-and-bottle-washing) for a while. People on big corporate ladders rarely gain that much diversity of experience. Part of our job, as the progenitors of Teamability, is to let people know that there's a way to discover who you are, and how you 'team' most effectively and happily, without risking the security of your family or future.

Your response to discovering your own Teamability could just as easily be "Now I know I would hate (or love) having my own business," as "Now I know why I hate my job - I quit," or "Now I know why I LOVE my job; no thanks, I'd rather not go into management."

Yes, there is the glass ceiling of reality, and a glass box of our own making. The important question: is yours opaque or transparent?

@DrJanice: Anger is an emotion, hostility is a way of life. (Your choice.) #justsaying

It's counterintuitive to think of something positive as negative, and vice versa. But really, once you get past that scorching hot wall of 'no' it's really quite satisfying to know that yes is just across the road.

The Positive Power of Anger

Anger is generally classed as a negative emotion, along with fear, sadness, and disgust. Like other overgeneralizations, this one leads many of us to believe that the answer to the world's ills is to eradicate, or at least control, anger. (As Machiavelli noted, it's much more empowering than a smile, but we'll leave him for another day, since we're not quite ready to take over any kingdoms.)

A very intellectual friend recently related a group discussion he'd had on the topic. He said that the focus was on anger as a purely negative emotion that leads people to confrontation, bullying, violent conflict, hatred, and even war. Sadder, there was shared pessimism that not being able to eliminate anger meant that there could be no end to terrorism.

I opined that pessimism comes from the rigidifying of belief that because the other person won't change, nothing ever will. Not much different than what goes on in stalemated marriages – or the typical dysfunctional organization, if you get my drift. So, of course, I wandered back mentally to my old days as a marriage and family therapist. (Understand, these were not 'good' old days. I've never enjoyed fruitless conflict, and there were times I had to assert that there was no way that I was going to be the person in the room who most wanted the relationship to succeed.)

But here's the optimistic part: anger can be positive, constructive, and the most human way to do business, whether that's personal business, commercial business, or what goes on behind diplomatic walls.

Seeing anger as a motivator or initiator of positive change is definitely a challenge for most people. That's because it's so often confused with hostility. Here's an easy way to get around that.

Anger, like pessimism, is just a feeling. It's situational, so you can use it as needed, and put it aside when it isn't your best strategy. By comparison, hostility is a way of life. It's a behavior, and like any other, it can easily sneak right into your list of habits. (Think: wash face, brush teeth, scowl.)

So why are you angry? You're angry when things are not going as you have planned. You've bargained with the fates, or someone important to you, or even yourself. You've done *your* part, but they haven't done *theirs*. The fact that you planned the whatever-it-is and they had no part in it, and you never guessed whether or not they would even agree with you, is the real source of the problem. Not to minimize the effects of that problem on you – the stress, the strain, the very uncomfortableness of it – the fact is, it *is* your problem. And that's the good news, because it's easier to fix things when you own them.

Often, if you can get close enough to an angry person you at least have an opportunity to 'move' them a little. (Once you have motion, you're getting somewhere.) You know how to do that. You approach them 'in neutral' and just listen. No confrontation. No showing your superior knowledge or authority. No nothing. Just listening. Because just like a kid who's having a tantrum, anger eventually burns itself out. And then, the other person's resistance drops. Not dramatically, but enough so that you can poke the embers a bit and see if something's likely to flare up again.

The interesting thing is, you can also do this for yourself when you're angry, even if you're angry beyond mere words. In fact, that's when it will be even easier, because it was the words – the non-negotiated bargain – that fanned the flames of anger in the first place. And it's listening that prevents that anger from hardening into hostility.

Because we (my friend and I and probably you, dear reader) are global thinkers who like to ask the really big questions we don't have the 'right' answer to, here's where our conversation led. We asked ourselves, how does the unbridled expression of anger impact world peace? And, being sixties people (peace sign!) we naturally followed it up with, is there anything we can do about it, personally, nationally, and globally?

I have no definitive answer. But I do know this.

Anger is an emotion. Hostility is a way of life. It's your choice.

@DrJanice: Chance favors the prepared (and socially connected) mind. Just updating Louis Pasteur.

There's a lot of data that says that women visit doctors more than men, partly because they're more likely to be escorting children and elders. What I really wonder about is whether or not people consciously think about how they partner with the doctor – and increasingly, their other primary and specialty care sources. (Special hats off here to nurse practitioners and advanced practice nurses!) Does that drive decision-making, or is choice a thing of the past?

Does Your Healthcare Culture Need to be Cultured?

Back in my 'mom' days, one of my big wishes was for a quick way to culture whatever it was that was colonizing my child's throat and causing complaints of pain and coughing. (By the way, I'm still a mom – I just don't hear the word 40 times an hour any more.) There were so many advantages to learning exactly what was causing the fever and, even more, knowing what to do about it. I figure I would have saved at least 70 rounds of unneeded antibiotics (average co-pay, $20), not to mention the constant worry that the wrong treatment could result in unknowable horrors, and ultimately, induction into the Mom Hall of Shame.

So when I was asked what could be done to improve the culture in health care institutions, I naturally thought about what I'd do if the entire staff came running toward me, each of them crying out in pain.

That isn't far from the truth.

When one of the most-read articles on Medscape.com is entitled *Why Nurses Eat Their Young*, the health care environment is clearly in trouble. And just like when a kid's getting a sore throat, it would be good to start by culturing the culture to find out what we're up against. But, unfortunately, you can't do it with a swab. Because the thing you need to culture doesn't exist inside a single 'patient.' It's what's happening between people. That requires a different method.

People – unlike bacteria, viruses, and so on, which can be notoriously difficult to culture – have much less stringent requirements for reproduction. (I am speaking of people's behavior now. Making babies while at work is clear evidence of a culture gone wrong!) Left uncorrected, bad acts – such as inattention to patient safety – can multiply until the level of inattention gets so high that patients and their families can't help but notice. Then it gets reflected in patient satisfaction scores and/or litigation. And that's just one example.

The good news is that strong positive human cultures also multiply. And that means that when you've identified the 'pathogens' you can begin the great cleanup.

Here are some quick ways to screen for a 'pathogenic' culture:

Do people follow the rules? This includes everything from hand washing, to coding visits appropriately, to respecting all clients regardless of how much grouchiness their infirmities may be engendering.

When they do follow the rules, are they following them because of their professionalism...or out of fear?

Do managers use creative ways to develop and support their teams and their individual reports?

Do those 'creative ways' include things like playing favorites and using HR's disciplinary process like a club?

When the situation grows more pressured (think 'Emergency Room in a war zone') do health care providers share the responsibilities without thought to the exercise of authority or 'getting credit'?

Are there 'silos' that only members of one group or another are allowed to penetrate?

When an error happens, do people generally try to understand exactly what went wrong before assigning blame?

Is the blame for problems always laid to one group or another? Perhaps even the patients?

Who has responsibility for preventing mishaps, miscommunications, misinformation, and other 'misses'?

Is your answer to the last question someone – or everyone?

Ultimately, the culture of a health care organization is revealed by the way people team together. Start with an understanding of what that means, a plan to improve, and the analytics to track it all, and you'll be on the way to a healthier culture!

@DrJanice: If you think inclusion is a good idea, make sure your actions are actually inclusive. #justsaying

Most people don't know that I once had a pretty active political life. I ran for office, got endorsed, wrote a lot, and those ideas got written about. But it was always the other part of the election process that interested me, the part that to this day I believe is in serious need of disruption. For everyone's sake.

What if We Gave an Election and Nobody Came?

Election Day comes every year. Wherever you live, you'll probably be asked a few ballot questions along with your selection of candidates for whatever job openings there are. Yours might be about your willingness to fund some project or change some tradition or underwrite some new bureaucracy.

Did you ever notice that these Election Day quizzes are always made up of yes/no questions? I've taught college and grad courses where essay questions are the norm, but it's taken me a while to understand what's been bothering me. We're cheating our electorate by only giving multiple-choice exams – with only two choices yet. We can write in candidates, but where we'd really like to give our opinions, only yes or no are acceptable. What's wrong with this picture?

What if, instead, this year's ballot had essay questions? Might that not produce a more solution-focused agenda? Perhaps it could look like this:

Public Question #1: What do you plan to do, personally, in the coming year to make your hometown a nicer place to live?

Public Question #2: How can we fund government so that no one individual or group feels put upon?

Public Question #3: Is our society a just one? Answer by citing three examples, pro or con, and analyze each within the context of domestic and foreign policies.

Now I know you're thinking:

a. I just don't have time for this.

b. I barely made it to the poll before it closed last year.

c. I didn't know we were having a test or I would have studied for it.

d. All of the above.

What if we gave an election and no one came?

Perhaps its time for us to take responsibility: for the future of our families, our businesses, and our world. Perhaps it's time to make participatory democracy a reality. Perhaps we need to stop making it so easy to vote and then to forget what it was that we voted for. What better way to do that than to ask citizens to go beyond merely pulling levers? What better way could there be to inspire the entire spectrum of feeling, belief, and thoughtfulness that our electorate is capable of, than to ask them to share it with all of us?

The pedagogues among you may ask how I plan to grade these essays, to determine which ideas are worthy. The answer is simple. When you take the trouble to seek more than a simple yes or no, you begin to listen in a new way. You discover solutions that incorporate the diversity. And eventually, you can give an election where most everyone comes.

@DrJanice: Engagement goes both ways. Do your people know you're engaged with them? #justasking

Sometimes I sound like such a curmudgeon, but really it's because it annoys me when people use numbers – or even 'science' – to back up their opinions. Not that opinions are wrong, you understand, but sharing a feeling, having an inclination, or even 'entertaining a notion' (the phrase with which one person of my acquaintance used to preface his orders) does not reach the pinnacle of TRUTH! And while truth in all caps is pretty hard to come by, can we all agree to at least try to get at it?

Why I Don't Appreciate Engagement Surveys

It may just be that I'm a lifelong entrepreneur. In that world, engagement is a baseline assumption. Why else would I have started that first business when I could have followed my peers into those bastions of business that guaranteed you the security of a cushy retirement? (In fact, at my age, any retirement.) And how could I have attracted my business partners, early employees, and those vendors who became like business partners, if we all were not sufficiently engaged?

Here's my problem with the explosion in popularity of engagement surveys, which ask things like '*Do you have the materials and equipment you need to do good work?*' and '*Are you able to do what you do best?*'

From my perspective, any given employee:

- May know (or think they know) what is expected of them and even think they are doing a great job, but in practice, be annoying, error-prone, imperious, or worse.

- Might have all the best materials and state-of-the-art equipment to do their work, and still do a substandard job.

- Could feel they have the opportunity to do what they do best, but have no idea at all what kind of work would feel meaningful and satisfying to them.

- Might receive praise frequently, but not necessarily the kind of praise that cuts through the noise because it addresses and respects the way they seek to serve team needs.

- May have a best friend at work, but one who is also a distraction, or a bad influence.

The list goes on...

It isn't that the questions are bad or wrong. It's that surveys like these are designed to record and quantify the way people say they feel about their lives at work. As former CEO of a few high and low tech companies, I can categorically state that I've never seen feelings track to outcomes.

So what do I appreciate? I want to know just three things. And I don't need your feelings on the subject, either. I want evidence.

Do you get to do stuff every day that makes a positive contribution to your organization?

Does someone let you know the value of that contribution?

Does that cause you to do more of it?

@DrJanice: There's a big difference between a gift from the boss and company property. #justsaying

Still being a curmudgeon. I hate honesty tests. Not honesty. I love honesty, right up there with transparency, openness, and a frank approach. But honestly, how do you pass those &/#%$ tests? Short answer is, start with the question at the end of this chapter.

Take My Pencil. But Please Leave the Computer.

I just read that, according to the U.S. Chamber of Commerce, 75 percent of employees steal from their workplace, and many do so repeatedly. Instant flashback to the day my neighbor showed up on my doorstep, lamenting that his kid didn't get a job because he had flunked the 'honesty test' given to him by HR. This is the same person who knocked on my door to confess to having caused some small mishap that I hadn't even noticed. In short: the most honest kid I have ever known. So much for honesty tests.

I was once president of a sheet metal manufacturing company. It was the kind of business where 'theft' meant someone had highjacked your truck and fenced the contents, so I'm sensitive about the various levels of what I prefer to call 'misdirection of corporate assets.'

Dr. Dan Ariely, behavioral economist and author of bestseller *Predictably Irrational*, has done dozens of studies on just how far people are willing to go in the direction of dishonesty while still maintaining a self-image as a 'good' person. So we have some reassurance from a distinguished researcher that it's forgivable to take a pen home from work, but not a box of them. But I found it a bit disturbing to realize that I've often been overly tolerant of bad behavior.

Here's the question: How do to tighten up the ship? Deterrents work very well. But only if all of these conditions are met:

1. Everyone needs to know that if anyone steals, something bad will happen.

2. They need to believe that if they steal, they will be caught and punished.

3. They need to see that punishment as truly undesirable.

I can see you shaking your head at that third one, asking yourself, isn't every punishment undesirable? Actually, no. The usual punishment for stealing things at work is getting fired. For some people, that's a reward, not a punishment. This is especially true if the person heads directly to the unemployment office and collects benefits because you didn't have the heart to fight it.

America's prisons are filled with people who: a) never thought or believed that they would get caught; b) thought that getting caught wouldn't be all that bad; or, c) just didn't care at the time. That's the problem. *It's truly rare that all three of the essential conditions of deterrence are present at the same time.*

So here's the question: How do you make sure your people are not among the three-quarters of the workforce cited as pilferers (or worse) by the U.S. Chamber of Commerce? The answer: You can't 'make sure,' but you can make improvements.

First, do a security audit and check on critical systems and processes in Finance, IT, and physical security. Remember: when you allow vulnerabilities, you create the other guy's temptations.

Second, know that most people do desire to be good, so take action to reinforce that orientation. One of the most effective tactics is to educate and improve management skills in reducing workplace stress. Why focus on stress? It's because uncertainty, verbal abuse, and unfair treatment makes people frustrated and angry. And when people are angry, one of the ways they work it off is to take things and self-justify that it's only evening the score.

Finally, take the advice you'll find on any typical investment brochure: "Past performance is not an indicator of future performance." Think about this when you invest your trust in people. Some of the best and most honest workers you can hire might have slept behind bars for a time, and learned the hard way that they never want to go back. It's called 'going straight,' and it really happens. Meanwhile, there are plenty of honest, respectable folks who might be just a bad mood or a breakup away from dipping into the till.

Now, getting back to that dad on my doorstep with the kid who flunked the honesty test. Here's what I told him...after first calming him down and citing chapter and verse on the virtues of his admirable and upright offspring:

"Would you really want your son to work for a company that doesn't trust him?"

@DrJanice: How do you build a #data scientist? My POV: start with a scientist. Physical reality rules. #justsaying

The genesis of this piece was a request from the always-compelling Steve Wilson, one of the stars of Constellation Research. (Actually, they call them analysts, not to be confused with the kind that always wants you on a couch and not peeking at them. Yes, I digress a lot.) Steve was in the midst of writing a report on privacy and consumer rights and asked for what's called a 'parallax view' – not necessarily an opposing viewpoint, but one that would provide an independent, different viewpoint. While I could not find a single thing to disagree with in his analysis, I was able to write something different. Which he graciously included, though I'm fairly sure it was not what he actually expected.

Privacy, Trust, Data, and Love

The near-complete annihilation of privacy can be a terrible thing. But when it happens between two people, the result is an extraordinary reward called 'falling in love.' So why, then, are we seeing such an uproar about something to which – under the right circumstances – we are so willing to surrender?

Perhaps the current conversation on privacy needs a refresh on the element of context. In this sense, context would include the set of limitations we put on the scope and depth with which we are willing to interact with a particular 'other.'

Using myself as an example, there are people with whom I will share the entirety of my self: not merely the quantitative, but also the qualitative. That's because, for me at least, it feels good to be understood, and to truly understand another person requires a high level of information, both historical and current. Further, there needs to be a high level of confidence that this information will be used in a positive way, if not for me then for someone or some thing we both care about.

And then there are entities with whom (or with which) I share selected information. They will never fully understand me, but they may offer me something I could not easily locate or obtain for myself. (Yes, if you have black t-strap kitten heels that I like, I will happily disclose my shoe size. But I'm not telling you my secret number – the price I'm willing to pay – because that makes for too one-sided a relationship.)

Lastly, perhaps sad to say, there are those with whom I will only share misinformation. If I sense a bait-and-switch, or an attempt to capture my information under false pretenses, I am likely to provide entirely fabricated data, chuckling to myself as I fool your system. I don't trust you because I learned that you don't have my interests at heart, and may even be opposed to them.

And so, I may trust you with my data, my information, my heart, and even my soul. But remember, I will always be asking one question:

Will you still love me tomorrow?

@DrJanice: Make sure your carbon-based life forms and silicon-based life forms can team well too!

Innovation: the final frontier. These are the voyages of your life. Your mission: to explore new ideas, to seek out new opportunities and new prospects, to boldly go where no one has gone before.

Team Well and Prosper!

It's your future. You can either go it alone – be the captain, first officer, communications officer, navigator, chief engineer, cook, and barkeep – or you can discover and develop your 'personal best' way to make team contributions, trusting others to exercise their mode of contribution with equal authority and responsibility.

Teaming in a new way with an entire team is a daunting challenge, with potential high costs and risks. It's like being newly born and all of a sudden having to navigate nursery school. Life doesn't work that way. We learn to relate to other people – to team with them – by first connecting with one other person, and then two others. Collaboration happens haltingly at first. (Think about the complications of getting along with parents or guardians. How long did it take you to figure out that you couldn't tell one of them something without the other, somehow, 'magically' finding out?)

So if you want to invest in better teamwork, your quickest ROI will come from finding a person – just one person – with whom you have a natural 'fit.' This is not a random match. The research that resulted in Teamability® tells us that for each one of ten specific modes of team contribution (known as Roles, with a capital R), there is a complementary Role. When you (with your Role intact) meet a person who is your 'Role-partner,' an instant connection will be made, and it will have nothing to do with age, appearance, gender, or intellect. It will be a naturally occurring synergy between your Roles that inspires, ignites, produces, distributes, or solves something, and creates value for the team.

If you haven't yet experienced Teamability, you don't know your Role, and that's okay for now. Just read that list again and let the words sink in. *Inspires, …ignites, …produces, …distributes, …solves.* Which one seems more resonant, more appealing, and more deeply meaningful to you?

Here's a first step toward discovery of the part of you than longs to team with other people. It works because the five words are essentially about the needs of a team. If you sensed a special connection to one above the others, then that word may be telling you something about the Role that exists within you.

Inspires

Your Role is likely to be a Founder or a Communicator – the Role-pair that gets people excited about a new mission. Do you have a big dream, or do you love bringing people together to support the achievement of big dreams? For a team to form, to innovate, and to do more than simply carry on, there needs to be a vision, and a means for communicating and maintaining the vision. When a Founder and a Communicator get together, that's what happens.

Ignites

The Roles of Vision Mover and Vision Former convert ideas and descriptions into strategic plans and activities. Have you noticed that you naturally take to being a spark plug in a group? Do the words 'here's how we're going to make this happen' ring a bell? These are power-packed Roles, but without each other's influence they can be like gasoline in a dish. One flash and it's over. Together they are like gasoline in an engine. Apply the spark and you can really go someplace!

Produces

Your Role is likely either an Action Mover – the deployment specialist – or an Action Former – the expert in detail and follow-up. Think of a team leader who keeps the troops burning through their to-do lists, and a project manager with a clipboard, checking things off as they're completed. Here's the essential Role-pairing: deployment without follow up can go seriously haywire, and follow up without deployment is pointless.

Distributes

If you are an Explorer, you may have noticed your knack for spotting valuable things or opportunities that others missed. (Like, all the time.) If you are a Watchdog, you probably have a natural interest in caring for the needs of others; getting those resources to the place where they'll do the most good. Explorers team from a distance, and Watchdogs team from within. As a pair, they provide an internal/external linkage and balance that becomes a lifeline for any kind of organization.

Solves

Every organization needs sources of information and applied ingenuity. People of the Curator Role will, all on their own, gather and organize massive amounts of information. (How big is your library, and how many trivia contests have you won?) Meanwhile, Conductors have a seemingly limitless appetite for tackling thorny problems. They are the ultimate fixers and greasers-of-the-wheels of production. (Do you feel that you don't get the credit you deserve? This Role-pair is a powerhouse of problem solving, but Curators tend to avoid the spotlight, and Conductors are often misunderstood by the people they help.)

In the end, understanding your own Role and connecting with your Role-partner will begin your voyage of self-discovery and personal innovation. When you no longer feel the pressure of being everything to everyone, you get to experience the joy of making personally meaningful contributions. Your own good feelings, and those of your colleagues, bring stress reduction to the whole team, which reduces friction and makes everyone more productive. Team players are neither dependent nor co-dependent. They're interdependent.

And that's how prosperity can be multiplied a hundred, a thousand, a million times over.

@DrJanice: "I'm more than just my own life. I'm also what I become with another – that third being." - BSP

Afterwords

I always like to have the last word on things. Sometimes, you just don't get to do what you want.

This section is titled illogically from a purely semantic view, but perfectly so from where I now stand. Because this section honors both the past – the memory - and the future – the ongoing value of the contributions made to Teamability® – by Barry, my husband of 33 years, who left this earth August 30, 2015.

Thus, two afterwords, not the syntactically proper, singular afterword.

The first is a eulogy, a farewell, a letting go.

The second is a small bit of advice, which I don't feel shy about giving. Unlike most generic advice, it works. That is because it springs from the tweet above. Which was taken from the very first letter Barry wrote to me.

It was very early in my thinking about how much teams and couples were similar. And it is proof – as if I needed any! – that he was there from the very beginning.

@DrJanice: The tighter you hold on, the more you trap yourself.

I have never been much of a manager. Even at home, where I needed to learn how to manage the kids' lives, the PTA cookie sale, and the occasional relocation, I pretty much learned to muddle through. Then one day I needed to make a lot of new decisions. And I realized that I knew how to do the most important management task of all.

Management – Like Love – Means Letting Go

I usually address bright, big picture topics, but this time circumstances have brought it very close to home. I hope you won't mind.

In the early evening of Sunday, August 30, 2015 after many years of declining health, my husband of 33 years went gentle into that good night.

Those who were close knew Barry as an incredibly loving person, but he was still quite able to rage against social inequalities and injustices – whether big (think slavery, 9/11, or Rwanda), or small.

He had no way to address holocausts, but he did have a constructive response to the slights and rudeness and dismissive behaviors he observed against those who could not fight back. And the fact that there were good reasons for not fighting back – potential loss of livelihood, or even life itself – is what truly raised his ire.

These days, a management consultant might praise Barry's approach as 'scalable, repeatable, and sustainable.' He simply showed people he cared. He modeled respect; not just tolerance. Even the most downtrodden would have his full engagement for as long as civil discourse continued, after which he would politely withdraw. And <u>that</u>, it turns out, was the greatest management lesson I ever learned: to withdraw. To be silent. To let go.

How often are management problems – like personal relationship problems – caused by the inability to just let go?

Case in point: I know someone who works in the innovation department of a huge company. The job description is, basically, find exciting and cool stuff, and report on it. So when I found an exciting and cool article on a very respected website, I sent this very hard worker the link.

I got an immediate response…but not the one I was expecting. It went something like, "<expletives deleted>, they won't let us access that site! Actually, most everything is blocked. Makes it really hard to do my job."

At some point – who knows when or why – someone decided that the company needed to control where people go and what they see on the web. Now that decision is obsolete and obstructive to the company's own desire to innovate and grow. And yet, no one is letting it go.

Just saying.

Personal relationships are much the same. Really, if you have to hold on tight to control your partner, how whole can they be? And how good is that for you?

A very wise person said to me, "When we are infants our hands are curled up; when we grow old, they are relaxed open." When I heard it, I thought, that is equally true of our maturity as managers.

In the end, there was no holding Barry back from his final journey. Even if there was, it's not the way he would have wanted me – or him – to manage it.

@DrJanice: All you need is love, said Beatles. But you need to keep the heart beating. #justsaying

We started our research with work teams, but I quickly realized that everything I really knew about them came from understanding how couples and families work. There are needs. There are resources. And with simply moving from thinking about one of you and one of them to 'us,' a glorious balance emerges.

Five Simple Rules for Making Love Last

People who are aware that I was recently widowed have been extraordinarily kind, in word and deed. Relatively few actually knew my husband, but many made warm and lovely statements about what kind of man he must have been.

It's brought me to the conclusion that the myth of perfect love is alive and well. And, unfortunately, it's probably doing more harm than good.

That said, Barry and I did have a long time together: thirty-three years, to be exact. Tightly bonded and on the same mission, we were a team. As a couple, we were a team of two. As a family, we were a team of four. In everything else we did together, we formed the core of a team that was dedicated to making something good happen. And yes, this degree of team alignment was totally predictable. (Teamability® even works on teams of two!)

But being aligned in our responsibilities and our objectives was not enough to have a great marriage, any more than hiring great people is enough to build a great business. The stresses and strains of everyday life continuously chip away at shared commitments. But fortunately, there are rules of behavior that can preserve and rebuild them. They are simple to state, and here they are – with just one caveat: they are much more difficult than they seem. But if you really want it, I know you'll try.

Feel kindness toward each other and act on your feeling every day. If you aren't feeling particularly kindly on a given day, make the extra effort.

Always think more highly of your partner than your partner thinks of him or herself. It's really important to have someone who dreams for us and believes in us, and most of us never got enough of this when we were children. Relationships are supposed to help us finish growing up, and nothing grows people better than someone believing in them.

Learn the emotional balms and bandages your partner prefers, and keep them on hand. When the outside world has caused them pain, and you need to do some first aid, you can care for them the way they like to be cared for. Soothing your partner's hurts needs to be done their way – not necessarily your way.

When there are pebbles in your partner's path, sweep them away quietly; if possible, invisibly. Before long, they will begin to see that their path is easier when they are with you than when they are not.

Listen to the way your partner is talking, and not just to the words. Whining, crying, moaning, and complaining all sound childish to the adult ear – because they are. You won't help your partner (or your children) to recover, or to grow, by resorting to the same behavior. Hold them, rock them, speak soothing words, and dry the tears. Then remind them of all their wonderful virtues and how they are growing every day.

Strong relationships have to be built over time, and the axiom 'No pain, no gain' applies to strengthening the 'muscle' of your relationship as well as your biceps. If you are so inclined, try treating other people in the same way and you'll also become a healing force in your workplace, your community, and the world.

Acknowledgments

It is always the team that I turn to when it is time to acknowledge just about anything. So consider this your reminder that no one does anything of true value entirely on their own, and let me count the ones who have been there, contributing to the mission of our organization:

- Dr. Jack Gerber and Mark Talaba, my partners and colleagues in broadening the path of innovation in teaming science, even as we dream of its far-off tomorrows;

- Our early investors, all people who understood the big vision, wanted to be part of it, and helped create the fertile ground to feed our Team;

- Our early users, companies and organizations at the leading edge of change – not only for their own profitability, but also for expanding their own big visions;

- Our channel partners, who learn, share, consult, and communicate, and through whom we reach more people, Teams, and organizations than we could ever find on our own;

- Richie Etwaru, Chief Digital Officer at QuintilesIMS and TEDx organizer, for suggesting the title of my TEDx presentation…which became the title of this book;

- Tom Talaba, Action Former + Conductor extraordinaire, for awesome proofreading and ongoing support;

- All those who are cited, either by name or not, in this book, including our friends at Constellation Research, who have helped us to be seen and to see where opportunities would be coming from, even beyond the places we had imagined;

- Our social networks who share with us and for us – even when we have never met IRL;

- The people of The Gabriel Institute who are here every day, making it a joy for me to contribute what I do, knowing well that through them, the Team's other needs will be met;

- And those no longer on earth, but still very much on the Team that lives on in my heart.

About the Author

Dr. Janice Presser is CEO of The Gabriel Institute, a behavioral scientist, and architect of the technology that powers Teamability®. She has studied team interaction in academic, clinical, and business settings for over 40 years, and has shared her expertise in the areas of HR metrics and measurements, workforce planning, and human capital assessment. Including *'Timing Isn't Everything...'*, Dr. Presser has authored seven books and myriad articles on various aspects of teaming, from parent/child, to personal and family relationships, to workplaces and spiritual communities.

In an era of digital disruption and transformational change, Dr. Presser's integrated technology and management methods are fostering collaborative cultures, generating extraordinary business results, and opening new pathways to meaningful work and organizational health.

You can learn more about the mission of Teamability in Dr. Presser's TEDx presentation. It's here: http://bit.ly/DrJaniceTED

Photo: Tom Thomson